DOMINIC NEGUS

WHAT ABOUT ME?

DOMINIC NEGUS

WHAT ABOUT ME?

As told to
Karen Appleton

Published by
Vivlia Ltd

Published by
. Vivlia Ltd 2023

A catalogue record for this book is available from the British Library

ISBN 978-1-909833-42-5

Printed and bound by 4Bind Ltd, Stevenage, Herts. UK

WHAT ABOUT ME?

LIFE DEFINITELY HASN'T GONE THE WAY I HAD HOPED!!!!
BUT I'M STILL HERE KICKING AND SCREAMING!!!!!

I PLAYED THE GAME THE BEST I COULD OF, WITH THE HAND I'D BEEN DEALT!

I COULD STAND HERE GOING HOW LIFE AIN'T FAIR AND HOW COME I DIDN'T GET THAT OR GOT THIS, BUT IF BEING TRUTHFUL AND HONEST, I'M THE ONLY ONE TO BLAME!!

ONE THING I KNOW ISN'T THAT LIFE AIN'T FAIR, BUT LIFE IS SO SHORT!!!

SO, I HOPE YOU ENJOY THIS BOOK AS IT GIVES OTHERS A CHANCE TO TELL THEIR TALES ABOUT ME!!! GOOD OR BAD, TRUTH OR LIES, WHO KNOWS AND WHO REALLY DOES CARE …………..

I DEDICATE THIS TO MY GIRL, NOT SURE YOU KNOW I HAVE A DAUGHTER, BELLA.

DAD

DOMINIC NEGUS

VI

This book is also dedicated to Mark Potter aka The White Shark, who sadly passed away before he got to tell his stories (probably a good job as none of them would have been able to have been printed).

I would also like to mention Ron Lewis who has also sadly left us but his story made the cut.

Both great men and will be dearly missed.

ACKNOWLEDGMENTS

Firstly, I extend a big thank you to everyone who took the time to contribute to this book. It would not have been possible to produce it without you all. I mention in particular Ricky Grover, a close friend of Dominic's for providing the foreword.

I am particularly indebted to the help and advice of the management and staff at 4Bind, Stevenage, Herts, for the printing and binding of the book. Likewise, I express my sincere thanks to Kevin Moore of KMDigital, Littleport, for his skill and expert advice regarding the design of the book cover and presentation of the photographs, all which have been provided by Dominic and people in this book.

Special thanks goes to Bob Lonkhurst and his partner Sandie Ball for their continued efforts to point us towards publication. Using his knowledge, expertise, kindness and patience, Bob has answered so many of my questions. As a self-published author of 10 books including a trilogy of "FIGHTERS FROM THE EAST END, the last of which will be published early in 2024. He has been a close friend of Dominic's for many years and I now consider him a friend of mine too.

FOREWORD

If I was to sum Dom up because people ask me to, he is a fighter. That's what he is. It's in his blood. The fight is not always about fists, sometimes it is demons and past regrets.

I was born and bred in the East End of London and the reason why Dom and I get on so well is because we came from the same sort of place, just not the same area. It was never about what exam grades you got, it was could you hold your hands up and fight. I am an actor and comedian but I couldn't read or write until I was 31.

I connected with Dom from the first time we met and that is why I agreed to do this foreword, even though I think the book is a get up haha. He just wants to see what everyone says about him so he can decide who to chin next haha.

Seriously though, there are probably a lot of things Dom would like to say but rather have his friends say it.

I would like to say Dom is the real deal. There is a lot of people out there who talk a good fight, but Dom would be the person who would hold his hands up and say "let's have it".

He has bundles of arsehole. He will fight anyone, anywhere, anytime, a bit like the old Martini advert.

I know this is going to sound ridiculous as most people just look at him on the surface, but you should never judge a book by its cover. Dom is quite a shy person who is also sensitive and caring. He is a fighter with lots of layers.

The most powerful side of Dom is his sensitive side, not the growler. You don't have to put up a front of how tough you are. I think though he is learning that. I think it is happening naturally anyway.

Although he wouldn't want to admit it because sometimes you have to keep that tough shell up otherwise you get people non-stop coming up wanting to try their luck. He has had enough of knocking people out. He just wants to live a normal quiet life now.

IX

Don't change Dom, be who you are, don't be afraid to drop your guard outside the ring, obviously in the ring keep your guard up.

It is an honour to have done this foreword.

RICKY GROVER

INTRODUCTION

Over a year of interviews and conversations, this is a book about people's experiences with Dominic Negus. This is the real person, not the person you may have heard stories about or seen on television programmes.

This book has been written with complete authenticity in the words of each person who has participated.

Yes, there may be some bad language, slang and other mishaps, but if you know any of the people you will hopefully be able to hear them telling their story.

By respecting peoples wishes, some have allowed me to print their whole name, some just a first name and others preferred to stay anonymous.

The good and the bad. The funny and the sad. The lover and the fighter. The fierce and the tame. The bullied to the trojan warrior. It is up to you to decide who he really is.

This book exposes Dominic warts and all.

I have known Dom for about six years now. I've heard many stories, and over the years have heard tales directly from Dom. That is not the Dom I know, and is why I offered to help him with this book.

The people in this book have all played a part at some stage in Dom's life. These are their accounts, their recollections in their own words.

As the saying goes never judge a book by its cover.
I know nothing about boxing or the security world Dom was in, but hand on heart every person who has agreed to be in this book and I have spoken to, have been nothing but polite and accommodating.

If half my friends were as honest and complimentary about me as they are about Dom, I would be very proud. The loyalty and bond that has come across is absolutely overwhelming.

Everyone has a past. Some still live in it, some try to forget it and some are haunted by it, but if every person could be as honest and turn their life around as Dom has, we would all be living in a better place.

A respectful, loving and well-respected man who is also the most doting dad there could be.

I wish you every success Dom and it has truly been an honour to be a part of it.

Thank you again to everyone who has contributed.

Do you know he has a daughter?!!

Here's to you Dominic Negus.

Karen

FAMILY

"It is all in the DNA"

BELLA
(Did you know he has a daughter?)

With me he is just dad. He is so caring and does everything for me.

Every time I meet any of his friends, they have never had a bad word to say about him. In fact, that's the first thing they ever say to me, that they could never say a bad thing about him. That makes me feel so nice to have someone, especially your parent, for people to speak about him like that. It's like he is my family member and people think of him very highly. It's really nice to know that.

My relationship with him is amazing. He is my best friend. When I was younger, I would do everything with him and go everywhere with him. I have a really strong relationship with him. I trust him. I can tell him anything, you know.

When we were in Egypt years ago, he kicked this really small man into the pool. This guy was always hanging around my mum and dad was like "mate, you need to leave it out" and he didn't, so dad kicked him into the pool.

I know about dads past.
The first and only time I have seen dad box was for the charity event this year. I was so nervous. I hated it. I was with my friend and she loves watching it. I feel when you are there watching someone else it's not so bad, but when it's your dad I was a bit like "oooo". I didn't enjoy it, but luckily it was over pretty quick. OMG I was so so proud of him though and the fact he did it for charity, for Mark Potter, was amazing.

I see dad every week, we normally just go out for dinner and watch telly and stuff. It's all very basic but I don't mind just sitting at home and being with him. It's nice enough for me.

It's very flattering that everyone knows about me, because dad is always talking about me.

I know people ask him to do talks about mental health and hope that one day, even though he loves doing it, he will stop with the boxing. The way he is on pod casts talking and being very open about his own mental health it would be nice for him, to show, especially men, that it's ok to have these feelings. I think he would be great if he could mentor and give talks to people about it.

I feel like boxing especially now is not worth it anymore, because he is older and has a bad hip, and I worry he is going to hurt himself.

I am so nervous about bringing my first boyfriend round to dad. He has made it very clear to me that he doesn't want me to rush, but he doesn't mind me meeting someone either. Most people are nervous to introduce a boy to their dad. I know he would be alright with it even though he will probably want to become mates with them.

I worry about him being on his own. When I am not with him, he is either working or at home. I think it would be really nice for him to meet someone so he is not always on his own. I know he has great friends and all that but it's different when you have a girlfriend.

I used to call him Big Bear when I was younger, but now it's just dad.

Dad, I am so proud of everything you are doing and love you so so much.

NIC
(Bella's Mum)

I was 28 when I met Dom. We met in Buckhurst Hill, he used to come into the café I worked at. I didn't know anything about him, nothing at all, didn't know who he was or anything about him.

I am being honest and I used to say that to him all the time and he used to say "yeah you did. I used to see you

2

looking at me". I honestly didn't even fancy him first of all. He used to come in with his friend, he is quite like loud isn't he, you would always hear him. I am not really like that. He used to come in and we just got chatting and stuff.

He said to me he remembers me going into Waitrose and I used to see him in there. Every day or whenever I was working he would come in and we got chatting, we swapped numbers and then we started talking. It wasn't normal, then nothing is normal with him, but it wasn't normal in the beginning either.

I'd start speaking to him and then he wouldn't speak to me. I now know it was probably because he was up to no good, doing what he was doing. But I didn't know anything about that, about him. Being honest if I did I probably wouldn't have got involved. I was in a bad relationship before that and there is no way I would have jumped out of that and gone into this. I would have probably run a mile.

As I said I was in a bad relationship before and the guy was terrible to me. Dom got in contact with that guy and I never ever heard from him again.

At that time, he was like the naughtiest of the naughtiest, but I never knew a thing about him. Then gradually we started seeing each other and obviously people were saying "Oh my god, you must be mad. He's this, he's that". But I take as I find and I got to know him and saw a different side to him. Like I wasn't in a good place, and he was good to me, amazing to me at the beginning to be honest.

He was all throughout, but he just has his mad ways, you know, and I'm not the most normal either, so me and him just clashed quite a bit. We are both Leos, both quite fiery and he sulks and I'm quite stubborn, so it just wasn't a great mix. That doesn't mean anything bad, he was amazing in the beginning, he swept me off my feet, like literally. He really did.

During my pregnancy he was really good, so proud. I hated being pregnant but he was always like "you look amazing". He's very complimentary I would say that. Every day he would tell me he loves me; he is a good lot.

You know what I used to say about him, he is just a good guy that did bad things. I would still say that.

He was there at the birth of Bella. He cried, God yeah, when Bella was born. All through when she was younger he was so hands on. He would change nappies, he'd feed her, he'd get up. He would wheel her in – we had a pink buggy - and he would, like he didn't care, he would just be proud pushing the buggy. You know a big guy like him, like some guys could be a bit like "oooh no", but he was very very hands on. I went back to horse riding and was at the yard quite a lot and he'd just have her. He was like "you go, I will take her". She went everywhere with him. He's a very good dad and still is.

He is an amazing dad. I would never fault him on that. EVER. He is a brilliant dad.

He has said, bless him, about us giving it another go but too much has gone on now and it is fine how it is. I get on with him, and like I say anything Bella ever ever needs, it is done. He is good so very good and I know I am lucky. When I speak to some of my other friends about how their dads are with their kids, I just always say to my mum I am very lucky. Bella is older now and Dom will still do anything for her.

There are so many words I could use to describe him. He is loving, he really is honestly, but always angry. Hot headed there is loads. Misunderstood I would say that too.

When I told him I was pregnant, I didn't know at that time he was facing a charge that could have sent him to prison. I so didn't know the half of it, at the time. Honestly now I do but at the time I didn't know what was going on. And he got arrested on a plane and I didn't know that.

With regards to the attack, I was pregnant at the time. I remember someone knocked on the door, one of his friends, and they said something has happened at the gym, something about it being burgled. They just told me a load of rubbish basically but it all came out after about what had actually happened. But I didn't know at the time, I really didn't. I got to the hospital and everyone was there and I really didn't know. I was a bit naïve really.

4

He has massively changed, he had to change, he didn't have a choice. Obviously Bella has a lot to do with that.

Dom has a lot of good qualities. He is generous and spontaneous to a T. He is very polite, sensitive and kind. He is loyal too. He has great manners.

With all that said Dom is misunderstood.

LORRAINE
(Bella's Grandma)

I remember the first time I ever met Dom, which must have been a good 20 years ago. He came into my house with Nicola, he blew me away with his bigness and the first words he said to me was "hello mum". I said to him "I am not your mother", which he totally ignored. We carried on talking for a good hour and a half after that. He kept referring to me as mum and I kept saying "I am not your mother, stop referring to me as mum". From that moment until now he has completely ignored it and still calls me it.

I love him, because even though him and Nic are not together he has always kept us in his life. He doesn't scare me, I don't care what I say to him and I do say whatever I want to him. We have a really good relationship with him. I feel he is always there for us.

I remember when we got burgled, he was straight here. He took it personally. We really do love him. He is part of us. That is the gods honest truth.

He is the best dad to Bella. He would walk on coals for her. He is a wonderful father.

He has the biggest heart. Both John and I feel exactly the same about him.

FREDDY NEGUS
(Brother)

We had a really good childhood. Our next door neighbours were Sarah, Ian and Paul. We used to play a lot with them and have a lot of fun with them down Ray Lodge Park, long summers together.

It was good fun. Then Dom decided at the age of 10/11 to take up boxing, he might have been a little big younger. Mum used to take him down to Garden City which is in Hainault, Essex and he learnt his craft there really.

I was very heavily bullied at school and so was Dom for a little while. I remember one day, it was a Sunday, we went down to our local sweet shop which was called Freddie's at the end of our road and Dom and myself were spending our pocket money on sweets, which we always did, and one of the school bullies walked in. He looked at me first and said "Alright Fred you fat cunt" he looked at Dom and all he got out was "Alright Dominic you fat" and that was it, he couldn't finish his sentence, Dom just fucking sparked him. It was like something out of a comedy show.

He fell into the bottom shelf of this shop which was bread and above it was all magazines and newspapers. As he hit this shelf all the papers and magazines just came down, cascading all over him. And pretty much from that day the bullying for him and for me stopped. It literally just stopped.

So, Dom went from being literally just a grave face in a big school to being a big face in a little school overnight. No one fucked with him, it was a given to leave Dominic alone, and even though he is two years younger than Fred, you leave Fred alone as well because otherwise you will get Dominic's wrath. You know these were people that were seasoned bullies, you know they knew how to get to ya, and it just stopped.

Another memory I have is I had a girlfriend called Ellie and she lived in South Woodford. Our mum and dad set curfews, say it was 11pm. I would go around and see her say two or three times a week, and I would always get the last train back say about 10.40 to Woodford Station and I would run all the way from the station to my front door, where my mum would be literally standing on the doorstep counting down the seconds. You know she was that strict.

I made it every night and this went on for about three or four months and Dominic must have been about 15 at the time, because I was 17. He said to mum I am going out this weekend and going to stay at a friend and she was like, "no you are not". He was like I am going, it's a friend's party and I am going to go. She was "it's my house my rules, and if you don't like it you can go". He literally went upstairs, packed a bag and went "See ya" and walked out the door.

That was Dom. We didn't see him for two weeks. He rocked up one day to get some clean clothes, and mum and dad begged him to stay and obviously he did and that was the end of my curfew!!!!

In that respect he was a real trail blazer, he took no shit, if it wasn't on his terms. He would compromise, he always compromised, he is a very compromising person but if it wasn't on his terms you can get fucked cos I'm gonna do it anyway.

He has always had that larger than life personality, but, he always took into account other people's feelings at the same time.

We went through a little stage where Dominic and myself, when we were growing up, it was the weekend it was pub, curry, fight. That was our weekend and we would fight anyone, you know what I mean.

One time we went to the local Indian restaurant, Dom was wearing glasses at the time, they were proper thick glasses. He had an anxiety about people talking about his glasses, real phobia about it, he didn't like it. There were two chaps sitting on a table.

Picture the scene. There was a long table with all of us sitting, a group of about eight or nine of us. I'm in the middle against a wall, stuck right there, and these two other chaps are on the table next to us and Dom gets this bee in his bonnet that they were talking about him. They weren't, but he gets this bee. After about three minutes they pay, they leave and I knew it was all going to kick off because Dom took his glasses off and ever so calmly placed them on the table. I thought "oh fuck", here we go. He has gone running out the door and I'm shouting out. I was with my ex-wife at the time, who was my girlfriend then and a load of other people. I'm shouting out "get out the way I need to help Dom, I need to help Dom". Anyway, I ended up jumping out my seat, running across the table and literally jumping out the door as it is closing, followed by another couple of pals. John Croney was definitely there as I remember he was wearing white jeans and as we were running to help Dom he slipped over and got all his jeans dirty.

But we ended up having a ruck with these two blokes. Dom is working on one somewhere and I am working on another over there. I am hitting this fella, I am hitting him so fucking hard and he is really taking it well and I just stopped in pure frustration and I've gone "will you please go down" and Dom has just run past, if you can imagine he looks at me with the biggest grin on his face, and as he runs past he caught this guy right on the chop, right on his jaw, and he dropped like a sack of shit. Dominic hadn't stopped running, hadn't even looked at the bloke, he is just smiling at me. It was something out of a scene from Fools and Horses. That was so funny. He would have been about 17/18 years old.

Another ruck I remember was at a pub in Woodford Bridge. I get a phone call, I had a baby at the time, my wife had just given birth to my daughter. I'm at home and I get a call from Dom saying "I need you up the Wheelers now, big trouble, there's a couple of us here, but we need to make up numbers". I'm like ok. I go to go to the car and my wife says, "I'm coming with you".

We go up there and Dom is in the car park with a couple of pals. They were in the car park and said "it's all good, it's not going to kick off, but if you can just watch us" as they were going to walk home and I was going to drive home. I said no problems. They left a couple of minutes earlier and I sat in the car park and said to my wife we will go now. As I started driving down the road I see my group of pals, Dominic included just walking down.

All of a sudden, blokes just descended out of nowhere. There were five or six of them just on them. They came out of bushes, round corners, they had obviously been waiting for them and proper ambushed them. I had gone

8

past them this time in the car, so I went into reverse, drove back, got out and basically just got stuck in. Dom was standing there. He's got one bloke on his back who is hanging off of him, whilst he is hitting another guy. The bloke on his back fell off but is still hitting Dominic in the back.

What Dominic didn't know was the guy that he was hitting, as he was hitting him his elbow was hitting the guy that was trying to hit him in the back. Honestly, he smashed his face to pieces. It wasn't just one, you see Dom is a quick puncher, the time it takes one person to give one punch he can get off three. He split the guys nose, lip and all his forehead.

I got stuck in too. The carnage, there were bodies everywhere. We were standing there. It was like out of a WW2 film. There were bodies, blood and bits of teeth everywhere.

The guy that started it, he ran off, he literally shit himself and run off. It turns out the guy that Dominic's elbow kept hitting in the face was the dad of the guy that had run off.

There was another one. Dominic and his mate Jay. They went out for a meal, another Indian in South Woodford. I'm working at Greggs the baker in Enfield and doing the night shift, night despatch. I get a phone call from Dominic saying "got a bit of trouble here mate, John's gonna come up and pick you up in his motor". I was like "no problem". He has gone "there is something you might want to use", he told me where it was and I thought that will do, it was just something to protect my hands, I won't say more than that.

John picks me up and we pull at the restaurant, it's in George Lane, can't remember the name, and me and John walk in and as we do Dom is walking out the toilet. He has looked at me and said "that's them". He literally just said "that's them".

They were sat by the window, on the left hand. He literally walked over to the table and poofed this guy straight in the face, I have gone to the guy next to him, but unfortunately as I've gone over the table I've managed to split his head open with what I was using at the time. He

9

has tried to kick me off, I have gone flying across the table and Dom was tackling the other two guys. The guys were literally trying to get John out in the street. They were literally dragging him out of the doorway. Dom put both his hands on either side of the door and was clinging on for dear life.

They didn't get him out, he managed to stay in the restaurant. The guy that I tackled, literally just walked up to me, I felt like a football, literally I could see it coming, where I was sat on the floor as I had had the wind knocked out of me, and this guy just went poof with his right foot straight into my mouth. It was a proper proper penalty kick. Needless to say, he split all my lip open, my gum and everything else.

I looked up by the counter where all the spirits were and this bloke Dom has picked on this, I mean Dom's a big lad but this guy was taller, not a big as Dom but taller, and he shouted at Dom "I'm fucking CID, I'm fucking CID, I'm gonna get you fucked". Dom looked at him and said "I don't give a fuck who you are" and knocked him spark out. It was like you may be a big guy but I'm still knocking you out. That was him, in the zone, gone.

It was like we just keep going till the end and work it out after, you know what I mean. That's how it was, get through it and work it out after.

The police rocked up as obviously the owners called them and because Dominic was a frequent user of the restaurant, they arrested the other chaps and let us go lol.

That was pretty much our adolescent bit.

I got home that night looked at my daughter and thought I can't do this anymore. I pretty much took myself away from all that then. I have had a few good ones, a couple of bad ones but on the whole we did alright together.

My wife and myself split up, we were both young, both made mistakes but I was really in love with her. Before that though I always said to her if we split up I could never handle you being with other men. I would have to leave the country, so I would be away from you, away from the situation. I would just go back to looking just after me, just worry about where the next mouthful of food is coming

10

from, where the next bit of money coming from, just take my mind off you. She was like "yeah, yeah whatever".

Anyway, as I said we did end up splitting up. It was a pretty horrible scenario cos she had met someone and was still living in our home in Broadmead Flats and I moved into a flat in Ray Lodge, which is on the other side of Woodford if you like. It literally was just a tv, a chair and a bed. That's all I had, that's all I wanted. I wasn't interested.

I remember waking up one day and said to Dom "I can't do this anymore, I've got to get away. It's killing me, it's killing me". Knowing that she is with this other guy, moved into my home, my kids are going to be calling him dad soon, you know what I mean, I really can't cope. He was like "what you wanna do mate?" I was like "I need to go, I need to go somewhere, somewhere I can work and just worry about me". He went "give me a couple of hours". He rang back and goes "Freddy I can get you an interview with my pals' friend in Tenerife".

I was like its only four hours away and I wouldn't be that far away from the kids so Tenerife will be fine. He was like leave it with me. Within a couple of days, I was out there. He sorted me out. Because of Dom, after the two weeks, I had to book two weeks holiday just in case I failed the interview, cos that's what Dom said "all I can get you is an interview, that's the best I can do, the rest is up to you". I was like that'll do Dom.

I had the two weeks there, had the interview, got the job, and on the back of Dom the owner or one of the owners sorted me out a place to live, a little car I could use to run around and everything I needed to feel comfortable out there.

I owe that all to Dom. I couldn't have arranged that, but Dom did it for me.

I met a girl in Tenerife, this was about 20 years ago, so I must have been about 30 years old. She owned a bar and a restaurant and we got fairly close so I start running it for her. I mean it genuinely wasn't a failing business but it was only ticking over. So, we have gone in and together we have put in a plan and it was coming on really well.

Business was thriving, we had good status in the community and everything was going very well.

It was in a place called Los Cristianos in Tenerife, the bar was in a little row of bars opposite the Hotel Aguamar. It's very much a family orientated bar, we invited kids in. I staged a kids group every week with the help of Aguamar staff.

They used to do a kids club, but they needed to use somewhere that had karaoke facilities and room to move around. I was like bring them over cos if you bring the kids over at night the kids will ask the mums and dads to come to us as that's where they go during the day. So, we would get the parents over in the evening. Its good business sense.

There was a bar down the road and it was notoriously rough, and two of the lads from there came up onto our terrace and were smoking weed, and I could smell it. I just walked up to them politely and said if you don't mind take your chairs around the corner, you can smoke your stuff round there and then come back to the terrace.

They took real fucking offence to this and started shouting at me "you don't know who we are, you don't know who we are. We are part of the bar down the road. You're fucked, your dead". Then they left.

This is the funny bit at the time there was a guy called Marco. He was allegedly on the run from one of the armies, he was part of an army thing and the rumour was he had done some pretty grim things.

I was on my own at the bar as my partner had gone to the UK to see her family, I remember I was just standing behind the counter, looking out and the bar was open, this was about half an hour after this incident and Marco has walked up and asks "Are you Fred?" and I said yes and he said "you are fucked" and walks off. I was like "Oh shit" everyone knows not to fuck with him and there I was marked.

I'm thinking what the fuck do I do? What do I do? The only person I could think to call was Dom. So, I phone up Dom, on my old Nokia telephone and he was like "you alright mate?" I was like "in a bit of trouble here mate" and I told him the story. He has gone mental over the phone.

An hour later this Marco came up and he goes "we didn't know who your brother was, we are sorry" and walked off lol. Dom had got on the phone to a friend of his who had gone down personally to the other bar and told them they have got no idea who that guy is up at the end of the bar, because they really didn't want to be pissing off him or his brother.

They all came in and apologised and must have spent thousands of euros in the bar, they did karaoke every night for a week, they bought everyone drinks every night for a week. This is the clout he had.

Dom might have been in the UK, but his name and reputation got me out the shit. Seriously, I have never felt so close to death as I did when Marco came up and said "You're fucked". I thought I was going to be up Mount Teidi pushing up fucking daisies, but Dom, one phone call and it was sorted. It was absolutely brilliant.

Whilst away I tried to contact my children for months and months but my ex-wife wouldn't let me. Dom said "do you want me to do anything?". Bless him there was nothing he could do. I know he was watching the kids, making sure they were ok. I know that and to him I am forever grateful.

Dom is so loyal, he's got such a big heart. He treats everyone as a friend until you fuck him off and then he will tell you what he thinks of you and it's up to you to put it right or not. If you don't want to put it right then that's it, you have blown your chance. If you take it on the chin and say "I'm sorry Dom, it's my fault" then he would give you a second go, but he don't suffer fools lightly.

That's a proper Negus trait. We don't suffer fools. We hate bullshit. If you turn round and say you going to do something, fucking do it. If you say you are going to help me out, then help me out, because we will help you out for as much as we can for as long as we can until we stop.

Dom has grown into a lovely individual, a lovely man. A gentle man. Obviously it's the only side we have ever really seen. When you get to see the real Dom, not the showman, when he comes down to see me, he walks through the door and the first thing he does is fall asleep. That fills me with a nice warm feeling because it means he is relaxed, away from the bullshit.

The making of Dominic was Bella, when he had Bella it all changed. He got smashed up in a gym once. A guy with an axe and a gun and what have you, everyone knows this. He came out to see me a couple of days after, stayed with me for a while to recover and the aftermath of that to see in real life was pretty shocking. It was horrendous to be honest and after that he took stock and thought I got a daughter now and realised that this person is the centre of his universe and that changed him. That changed him.

With us he was always a gentle giant anyway but to see him come out of that horrible world was a relief you know because we all knew what he got up to but he didn't say anything about it. It has been documented on TV and in books and stuff like that, but as a family we didn't really know about it at the time and I mean when you watch Danny Dyer and stuff like that it glamorises it a bit.

I don't think there is anything glamorous about it at all I just think it was Dom trying to earn a few quid to get by. There is an awful lot of people out there that took advantage of it. They took advantage of his good nature and that Dom needed some money to survive.

Now that he is out of it, he can see the good from the bad. He is able to make that decision, but when you have only got one person paying a wage you only have to be loyal to one person.

Dom is surrounded at the moment by a couple of really, really good friends, that are like family to him and I feel safe in the knowledge that they have his back. You know I'm not going to live forever and I need to know he will be alright. Dom is a hard, hard person but his heart is really soft.

We lost mum nearly 11 years ago and every Mother's Day I get in touch with Dom to make sure he is alright. Every 9 July, mum's b'day I do the same too and also on 26 November dad's b'day.

Even after all these years he is still grieving them both. It's getting easier for him but on his bad days he has some really really dark days when he is really missing mum and it really does affect him quite heavily.

I do worry about him but am glad he has his friends that have his back that he can talk to. Dom when he is fucked up, is fucked up. He is a destroyer of worlds when he is in that mood and it is full self-destruct and I'm taking everyone with me. He gets a right head on him and then in a day or two it passes and he calms right down. So, it's good he has people to talk to that can talk him down. It's nice that Dom has those people in his life now.

Now that he is out of that world he is able to say "you stood by me, you stood by me and all the rest can go fuck themselves as you took advantage of me". He has a couple of good pals at the moment I won't name names but Dom knows who they are and obviously we have the group from back in the day Dom, me, John Croney, Jason Tann, Jason Burton, Danny Wright. We all got families now and it's gone a bit wayward because life takes over but we have a WhatsApp group and every now and then someone posts something to make sure everyone is alright.

DOMINIC NEGUS
(Nephew)

One of my first memories was when I was living in Tenerife with my dad at the time. I was 10/11 years old. I was in bed as it was a school night, all of a sudden, it must have been about two in the morning, my uncle Dom walks through my bedroom door. I loved my uncle as a kid, I still do, but I couldn't believe he was there. I was so happy to see him, I got up.

This was the time he was doing a runner for something naughty. I didn't know that obviously at the time. In the morning he and my dad walked me to school, I was so happy. He said to me he was going to pick me up after school, but he never did as he came back to the UK to face the music. I was so upset.

Another time when I was a kid I got arrested and got put in Ilford Police Station. At the time I was rowing with my mum so she wouldn't come and get me and my dad was living out the area, but my uncle came and picked me up. I got in his car. I was about 14 at the time and started to cry. He started laughing at me. He was laughing as I had got arrested and found it funny. He took me back to my mums and I had an argument with her and punched the door.

He instantly grabbed me by the throat and lifted me up right against the door. It was all about showing respect.

Obviously me and my uncle have the same name. I have never used his name for anything but I have hundreds of people that ask "are you THE Dominic Negus?". I'm like "no, I'm his nephew". Everywhere I go I get it. At work someone will clock my name, and it's weird really, because people are quite spineless because as soon as they find that out I get nothing but respect from them, which I probably wouldn't have got before that.

I have had it so much throughout my life. But as the generations go on it is getting less and less.

I didn't really know anything about Dom's life as a kid. Yes, I used to go to his fights but it was only when I read his first book "Out of the Shadows" I found out things I never previously knew.

I didn't know the half of it if I was honest with ya, but that's how he wanted it. To keep me out of that. As a man myself, I am 31 now, growing up you experience all sorts, especially growing up in East London.

He is a great uncle. Apart from that one story I told you, I have never had an argument with him. It is the only time that something like that has ever happened. Me and my uncle get on like a house on fire. We are quite similar. We take the piss out of each other. I have a special relationship with him if I am honest with ya, if you know what I mean. I am named after him. He truly is a great uncle. I wished I had spent a bit more time with him growing up but that's life.

He has had his problems and I have had mine. I was in care. I wasn't the best-behaved kid, but yeah I would have liked a bit more time with him, but we are trying to make up for it now.

My uncle knows this, but when it comes to Bella I feel that I have let her down. I am the older cousin and should really make more of an effort. I love her to bits, but I should make more effort to see her. I will always love and protect her and am here for her if ever she needs anything. She just needs to call me and I would be there.

He has so much energy about him now and he can't sit still. If you knew what he does on a day-to-day basis it is amazing that he can still be restless.

I get a lot of qualities from him, people even comment that our mannerisms are similar in certain things we do.

He's a great uncle to me and I know that like I do him, he loves me very much.

TRUSTWORTHY *Sensitive*

THOUGHTFUL MISUNDERSTOOD

LOVING KIND

BEST DAD RESTLESS

VERY CARING BOLD

BIG LOYAL

STUBBORN

Emotional FUNNY

INTERESTING

GUARDIAN ANGELS

"Anything is possible when you have the right people there to support you"

HENRY
(Entrepreneur and Close Friend)

I have known Dom from a teenager to the man he is today, over 30 years, with all his different stages of his life.

He was a gangly/skinny young man of 18 years. It was circa 1992 the days if you remember when all shops and retail outlets were closed on Sundays. People generally were quite bored. We were part of a company that would organise weekend sale events in hotel and exhibition halls. We sold household goods ranging from dining tables chairs, sofas etc.

It was hard work and a seven day a week occupation. Dominic would drive from our London depot as far and wide as Scotland, Wales, Devon, etc and set up the exhibition. We were on a tight time-table because we did not have access to the exhibition centre until midnight.

You would open at 9am in the morning for people to attend. These events were very well attended. Whilst the sale was taking place throughout the day we were constantly selling articles that were on display. These items needed to be delivered. This meant that the job was never ending and over weekends could be 16/18-hour days. Definitely not a job for the work shy!

It was at this period he got serious about boxing and literally I would hear him in the morning after he had been up all-night working fathering than resting and catching a quick sleep he was straight on the pads, to the point we would have to say "go outside to do that as everyone can hear and we have clients and are trying to sell". That went on for a couple of years.

After that period, we lost touch and then he went to another world, a dark world which is something that is not a part of my life. I was hearing stories. We did keep in touch but very occasionally.

We reconnected years later, when he decided to a step back, he had a terrible encounter that made him see what he was doing was not going to end well! When he came to that conclusion I discussed and would keep mentioning the benefits of being a good human being. I helped point him into the right direction.

Finally, a few years ago, I had I believe the ideal job for him. We manage hostels, and these hostels are the last safety net for a lot of people that have become homeless, lost their way in life or suffer from mental illness. They are not bad people but can be unbalanced.

Some of the homes have 140 rooms, I remember as we drove there Dom was like "no, I can't work at a place like this". I was like "we haven't even gone in, so why don't we go in and just give it a go. Nothing ventured, nothing gained".

He did, and now when you look at him now, he will chat to these people who can be unreasonable, mentally not well, but Dominic talks to them and tries to show them the right way. If they are struggling with their housing or income he will help them. He brings his life's experiences to. For example, if someone has been getting upset, angry, he sits them down and talks sense to them. It is an amazing thing from where he has been to where he is now. It's a complete turnaround and for the good.

The person I met was initially kind, then he went off and did his own thing, he is now back to the person I first met. It is true, so much so, he genuinely has a heart of gold.

He is extremely soft. In a business world he would get eaten alive, fortunately he is not in the business world.

When Bella was born that was the point of turning his life around.

Bella his daughter is his reason for living and being. We are trying to wean him off and make him understand that she is a young woman, she works very hard. He should and is very proud of her. She is going forward in life on her own path. I would like to be a fly on the wall when he is introduced to her first boyfriend.

What you find is he relives those days and has big regrets so much so that he beats himself up, this has to stop. He has earned the right to look forward now, not look back and stop beating himself. He is doing an immense lot of good now and should be content with that.

MARTIN BRISTOW
(Friend)

I originally met Dom from many years ago when he used to do the doors. We really got to know each other properly when Henry got married, which was about 11 years ago. From there on we have become the closest of friends.

At Henry's wedding we were going on a car tour up the mountain. I had got paired with Dom and we had a little MG convertible. I am about a quarter of his size and I remember him getting into the car and it started leaning over. It was a bit like a scene from the Flintstones, so funny. We had to go all up the mountains in this car. I was driving, literally he could just about fit in the car.

Dom has always been there for my family, he really would do anything for us. When my Tom used to play rugby, he helped him with his injury. He put him through training and helped with his recovery.

My daughter used to be a show jumper. We had horses and trailers. I remember we had a brand new trailer nicked by some travellers in Harlow. I offered a reward as wanted to know where it was. The reward was taken by them, then they told me they had already sold the trailer on to a guy in Clacton. I managed to get his number and called and asked if he still had it for sale to which he was like "no I have sold it". I told the guy it was my trailer and had been stolen. The guy then started threatening me telling me he was going to burn me house down. I was like, "ah ok, I have your address so I will be down there this afternoon to come and see you".

I phoned Dom up and told him what had happened. Dom and a friend went round there to see the guy.

Picture the scene, the bloke came out of his house, Dom and the friend literally only got out of the car, the bloke saw the size of them went white, panicked, turned round and legged it back into his house like the speed of light. It was hysterical, all they had done was get out of the car. We did get the trailer back.

I talk to Dom all the time. We all love him and he loves all of us. We see quite a bit of each other. We always go to dos together, to the boxing. We both know the same people, it's great. He is always around.

He is so proud of Bella, and so he should be. He has raised such a lovely girl. He is a good dad.

He really is just a happy go lucky, nice gentle giant bear. He has brilliant banter too. With Dom loyalty is the key. He loves his family and friends to bits and they love him just the same. He is just a lovely person.

You hear all these stories about him from his past, but I can honestly say I have never experienced anything of it. He has always only ever been there for me.

KEVIN (the Turk) GREENWOOD
(Greenwood Gym Owner and Friend)

I spent a lot of time in Tenerife. When I came back to the UK I was boxing and a friend of a friend introduced me to Dom. It was about 2008/2009. I got taken down to see him at the Sparta gym on the A406 before it moved to Chingford.

I walked in and there was Ian Wilson and Dom. We said hello and I told them I had had a couple of boxing bouts in Tenerife and now wanted to get into it and take it seriously and learn.

Dom said to me "do you fancy a move about?" which is another word for sparring. Me, being naïve, and wanting to impress was like "yeah, ok, lovely". I didn't really know what I was letting myself in for. I got into the ring with Dom and that was the first time I got my nose broken basically.

Ever since then we became the best of mates. He took me under his wing.

Where I had been away for so long, I didn't know of Dom or what he was like, his reputation, but when I met him he had this aura about him. This big character.

It was only when I got to know him and other people around him I got to really know about his reputation, but to me I only saw the other side of Dom. This other side of him that not many people know about or get to witness. That loveable fun side of Dom.

He is the hardest man I have ever met or known, but he is also one of the most loving, caring and compassionate people I know as well.

He trained me for 14/15 unlicensed bouts. I was training with him when he fought Chris Bacon in Manchester and Danny Williams. We were in each others pockets. We trained together, we worked together. He got me work doing the security on the boxing shows. He used to stay round my house quite frequently.

He is 12 years older than me, he was like a big brother, trainer and mentor all in one. I owe a lot to that man. I owe being a pro boxer to him. I am a trainer now, I train kids to box. Everything I know is down to him. I teach the way I was taught by him. The ways I deal with things now are due to things he taught me. As I said he was like my big brother. I never had a dad around me so Dom was the strong man in my life at that time. I love him dearly.

Everyone knows or have heard of Dom, but they don't really know him. When I have spoken to people who I have just met and they ask me who trained me and I say Ian Wilson, Lenny Butcher and Dominic Negus, though Dom was my main coach/trainer. Some go "Cor, what a nasty bit of work, I wouldn't want to cross him". I always think, you don't really know the real him.

Even though my memory is a bit hazy, what I do remember was every time you went out with Dom there was something to talk about the next day.

I do remember there was a Christmas party, we had it in a tapas bar. We had started early and been drinking all day, oblivious of the time. We weren't usually big drinkers as we were all training. We had completely lost track of time. There was a bar/club across the road and we decided to go over. There was about seven of us. As I said, we had been drinking from very early and we thought it was about eight or nine pm but it was really one or two in the morning. The doormen didn't want to let us in as they were closing.

Where we were all so drunk, we all just pushed our way in. When we got in there that was one of the times where you could really see what Dom was about. If anyone went anywhere near him he had the midas touch. Anyone he was hitting was going straight over. It went off royally. One of our friends kicked another of ours up the arse because he thought he was one of the other lot. It was like a Carry On movie.

Another Christmas party I remember was when Micky one of the other trainers started really well giving a speech. He probably had had a bit too much to drink but the speech then turned a bit sour. I can't remember exactly what was said, but Dom didn't like it and the next thing you know, Micky was asleep (laughs). It didn't turn out too well for him.

Dom after these events he is like "oh no, I've done it again" sort of things. Even though Dom has this stigma around him a lot of the time he is not proud of what he has done. He can laugh things off and generally speaking so can most people. Things amongst us never really get dragged out.

We all know with Dom to expect the unexpected.

Dom is the most loving dad. We used to always go out, me him and his little girl Bella. She is an adult now, driving a car. It's scary how time flies. That's still hard for me to fathom cos I remember going out when she was 10/11. The three of us going to watch the wrestling together, or going out for something to eat. He is a brilliant dad, a strong dad. He is a fun dad. I always say dads are for fun, mums are for comfort. He always had Bella in fits of giggles.

Dom is a very complicated person with his own mental struggles, nothing outrageous. I understand the method behind the madness of him. It is nothing vicious or nasty.

There are definitely two sides to Dominic. I think I am one of the lucky ones that know that side. He doesn't open that door for everyone. You always know where you are with Dom, there are no smoke screens or mirrors with it. If he is happy with you he is happy with you and if he is upset with you, he is upset with you. That's why you can always trust him.

STEVEN HEAD
(Headline Security)

I have known Dom since we were at Senior School. Dom went to a rival school and we knew he was a bit of a handful then.

I think we started working at the same security company doing boxing and gigs, which we both progressed through the ranks. We became friends. He has a great sense of humour and was someone you could rely on if anything kicked off. Great times.

Dom started boxing at 20 or 21 and really enjoyed his amateur bouts which we usually all went mob handed to the local Indian restaurant after.

Dom then turned professional at boxing and I split and started my own security company working for Frank Maloney, Frank Warren and Panix Promotions amongst others.

I remember I had a meeting with Frank Maloney, his brother Eugene and Dean Powell (Matchmaker).

At this point Dom had gone completely up in the underworld and had developed a big reputation. I asked them if they would consider signing Dom. They all agreed and knew they couldn't fuck him about. That was a big compliment as Eugene was not to be messed with himself.

They did sign him and Dom continued to have success in his boxing career.

I really didn't know much about Dom's personal life around this time but I did fall out with him over a security guard who worked for me and who Dom had become good friends with.

This bloke was a Walter Mitty character and everyone realised it after a while as he caused quite a bit of trouble with my work because of the constant lying.

Everything got back to normal soon after and I have carried on my friendship with Dom to this day. Business definitely not affected and Walter Mitty is a no one again.

I believe I will stay friends with Dom all my life because I honestly really enjoy seeing him and have a great laugh. 38 years mates.

TERRY ONEILL
(Security Consultant)

I first met Dom well over 30 years ago. He was about 19 years old, skinny, blonde curly hair and glasses. I also remember he never stopped moving. He was always bouncing around, chatting away. I was in my mid 20's.

Dom always wanted to be in the mix. If something was going on, whatever it was, Dom wanted to be front and centre. I remember when Dom told me he was boxing, I said, "whatever Dom", not thinking much of it. Little did I know where it would take him.

I worked with Dom in the security game on and off for the next 12 years. During that time, we got into a few sticky situations. Dom was always someone you wanted on your team, next to you. At times he wandered off and did his own thing.

That's the time he gained his reputation.

Funny thing is, all these people looked at Dom in a very different way to me. I never looked at him as the hard man. He was just always Dom, my mate, as he will always be.

I've read and heard about some of the things that have gone on over the years and its always upset me, knowing that that is my dear old friend. I look at him and I see a man who went down a path at times that maybe he didn't really want to, but when you get a reputation it's hard to let it go.

Having Bella was the best thing that ever happened to him. It gave him something to fight for, not in the ring or on a door, but for love. She's kept him going, that and the fact that I know the Dom that is underneath what people see.

I was back in London about four or five years ago with my wife and girls. We went to Winter Wonderland and it turned out Dom was there with Bella. We finally found each other and it was amazing. It was only for about 10-15 minutes, but it had been a long time since I'd seen him and you couldn't take the smiles off our faces.

We keep in touch. Drop a line every now and then.

I had my own troubles back then and Dom was one of the very few that stuck by me. I'll never forget that.

Dom is someone I will always regard as not only a friend but a brother. Love him dearly.

KEVIN MITCHELL
(Former Southern Area Title Challenger)

I have known Dom for about 25 years through the boxing. I remember we sparred at the Henry Cooper. I got on with him and we were the same weight, so obviously, and eventually was going to end up boxing each other. We had two great fights.

The first fight I beat him, to be honest I think he had things on his mind. It was hard to beat him as he was a top contender.

We then boxed for the Southern area title and Dominic beat me on points. The second fight took a lot out of me.

Both of our fights were seen by many hard-core boxing fans as two small hall classics by two very good and decent professional boxers. Two honest pros.

Then we had a third fight years later and he won the unlicensed section. As I said the two fights before were good fights but the last one he blew me away, he was too powerful.

More importantly with them three fights where we left things in the ring, obviously leave a bit of sorrow in the ring too, but them three fights made us become good friends, close mates.

He will confide in me and I'll confide in him and I know as a man he is a proper man. You know there are guys out there who think they are men and this and that, but I know he is a man. He has done his boxing and all right he could have gone further, but he has lived a life and he looks after his daughter.

I only have good things to say about him and I always message him once or twice a week to see that he is alright.

We recently met up and when we did, it wasn't to fight it was to give each other a hug and a cuddle. We had a soft drink, a bite to eat and a good catch up.

He is a good good man. He has a heart of gold as well. A lot of people won't see that but as the old saying goes "you don't have to show your heart to everyone because some people will take your kindness for weakness". Dom truly is a top man with a heart of gold.

NOEL TIERNEY
(KO Gym Owner)

Dom was my trainer and my close friend, not only did I box for him, he got me work as well doing some door work with Frank Warren.

I will never forget this time I had nowhere to go on Christmas day, I wasn't bothered but he was bothered. Anyway, what he done, he insisted that he took me to Nic's house, then to her cousins' house for Christmas dinner and made sure I didn't spend the day on my own. He basically come to my house, picked me up. He wouldn't take no for an answer.

This is what type of a guy he is, a kind hearted man. I didn't care I would have been on my own, but he wanted to do a kind thing. People don't know that side of Dominic and people should know this side of him, that he has a very kind heart as well.

I will never forget that what a lovely man to do that for someone.

He also used to pick me up for training every day at 5am and say "taxi for Noel".

What a lovely lovely man.

SPANISH MARTIN SPICER
(Friend)

I meet Dominic, it must have been over 10 years ago, when he came to Spain and we was training in the gym, boxing training. Obviously, I knew of him, but didn't know him. He came in with a few people I knew and he put me on the pads and he said to me "Yeah not bad. If you fancy a fight you get in touch with me and I'll sort it out for you", lol. I'm going back lol, I was 50 then.

Then he came over a few years later with his boxers. His young boxers that he got, Ben, Sanj and Hamzah, who is still fighting now, he took the title off of Spitz. There were a few other boys, but I can't remember them all. I used to go in the gym with them and he asked if I could give him a hand, just training them up as he had three or four at a time. It was really good and we got on really well.

He has taught me a few things about boxing as well. A few tips here and there.

I think with Dominic if he doesn't like you, excuse my language you can just fuck off and leave me alone, but if he likes you he will pull you into his company and he is a lovely man.

There is nothing, I haven't picked up anything bad about him in all these years. Obviously, he has his past, that was his job, but he has never been like that with me.

There is a funny story about him. There was a gym in Chingford and next to it there was a little café. In the café there was a chocolate cake that was past its best and the girl was just about to throw it out and Dominic said "Oh give me a slice of that, don't tell anyone ".

He's gone back into the gym, smeared it all round the toilet seat and on his hands and all that. Come out and says "Whose done this?, the state of it, it's all over the place!!!!". He had it on his hands and started eating it. Everyone went "UUURRRG" then obviously realised it was the cake, but the way it was done, was hilarious. He has a great sense of humour.

I am sure he has told you about his daughter. She is his world and that is it!!!

You know when you are in his company you will have a good time. He is a very nice, sociable friendly man. Obviously the other side if you upset him ……

I always have got on well with him and still do. He is a lovely man, I have got nothing but good to say about him. I have always seen the good side to him.

Whenever I came to England, he always got me a ticket so I could walk the lads into the ring with him.

Once he is your friend he is a lifelong friend. He is a great bloke - don't tell him that obviously lol.

JAMES SMITH
(Former ABC Boxer)

I first met Dom at 5 Star boxing club about 20 years ago. He was always a very big character, big presence and a really good boxer. I had two brothers, we all boxed. He is a bit older than me, but I always knew of him and his reputation from going to different clubs and being around different areas like Hollywoods, Epping Country Club and Atlantis. Even though we have known each other for a good 20 years we didn't go out together but always acknowledged each other. We all just knew the same type of people. I always saw him around.

Everywhere I went his name was mentioned "Dom did this, Dom Negus did that, he knocked out 3 doormen". You would go to a club and the doormen were scared of him because of his reputation.

The man can hit, he can bang with both hands. I have done boxing for many many years but he is a good boxer.

He is a good character, a good person. You obviously hear of all the stories. Dom's reputation was always in front of him all the time, it really was.

Somebody owed someone money and they asked Dom to retrieve it for them. He said he went to where he was told to meet them and there were two fellas sitting there and it turned out Dom knew them. One of them turned to him and said "Dominic, why don't you put some weight on??" as soon as he finished that Dominic went "whack", knocked him out.

It was because the guy was taking the piss out of him and that is one thing he just won't stand. Anyway, after that the guys paid up and Dom said it was done nice and easy.

Sadly, my dad passed away five years ago and Dom knew him too. So, he has always kept in touch sporadically. However, after seeing him recently at Mark's Potters funeral we have properly reconnected and message every week, just seeing how each other are. I have had some mental health issues, Dom suffers with his problems, we both have our demons. We now meet up every Friday and for a couple of hours chatting about things.

I lost my brother Danny 16 months ago who used to spa with Dom. When I saw Dominic recently and we got talking about family, kids and life Dom said to me "out of all the boxers I have sparred with your brother gave me the most agg. He was so awkward". That for me was the most amazing, lovely thing to hear and for him to say. You know Dom is a true professional when it comes to fighting in and out the ring so that was a lovely thing.

With Dominic you have your two sides, on a knife edge you have your bad Dom and then you have the loving Dom. He is a true family man. All he cares about is his daughter Bella. He idolises her like I do with my daughter. We just sit and have a lovely chat about the kids, family. We sit and put the worlds to right really. Dom and myself are still of the gentlemanly nature. You look after your family, you respect people, be polite to people, you open the door for ladies, sadly these days are gone. The world changes but helping and being nice to people makes you feel better about yourself.

He is such a big man, such a big character and nobody actually sees "you", they just pre judge you, they don't even know you. But when we are sitting down, we are probably two of the nicest most caring people you would ever come across.

Our hearts are in the right place. Yes, we might have done wrong in the past, got into certain situations, we all know Dom has, but his life is Bella. Everything is Bella.

We both get each other, we can relate with one another. We both agree our children keep us going. It gives us our fight and our strength. Because to be honest if it wasn't for them what is the point.

If you hurt his daughter or his family..... watch out.

I won't tell him this, but he is a real big teddy bear. In fact, I gotta tell you, he likes sprinkles on his latte. He expects me to ask for them when ordering his coffee lol.

Imagine two bald men, both that train sitting there, with coffee with chocolate sprinkles. We do get some funny looks from people. We both sit there talking about our children, how much we love them, what we would do if anyone crossed our children. Talking about life, how hard it gets as you get older, you know, your body falling apart from wear and tear.

Even recently he called to say "James I am so glad we are in proper contact with each other". I personally believe in life everything happens for a reason. People come in and out of each other's lives or re meet up when the time is right.

We both help each other we both talk about things we might not discuss with other people about. We open up to each other. It is a really nice friendship we have.

I would help Dom as much as I could. He is such a nice person. People don't see this. He has such a big heart. Caring.

He is tough. Obviously I have heard about the incident with him at the gym, the guys with choppers, he somehow managed to take it off them. It says it all really. Dom will admit that was the stage of his life where things changed. He knew his life had to go one way or the other and thankfully he had Bella. She saved his life and probably a load more other people's lives too.

Dominic now has to do what is best for him and Bella and what makes him happy. He has to look after number one.

Sadly, people used Dom for him to do certain things for them, because where are they now. They are nowhere. They don't give a shit.

Dom is very old school, old fashioned, like myself. Back then if it needed to get sorted you would meet in a car park and punch it out. Nowadays, it's a person who would stab you from behind and then throw acid in your face. It's a completely different world. The youngsters these days have no respect, no morals, nothing. It's a sad world.

Boxing is so important. It really gives you focus and respect, especially for kids who haven't been shown the way at home.

RON NASH
(Australian Entrepreneur and Friend)

I first met Dominic Negus late May 1995 before the Kostya Tsyzu/Ricky Hatton fight at the MEN Arena.

I had heard a few stories about Dom and knew he was a hard arse then as he was on of Kostya's bodyguards.

After many midnight calls over the weeks to follow Dom opened up to me just a little bit. I could tell there was a softer side to the big fellow and I could see he was a wonderful human being. He was also very contrite with his past.

Dom and I went through his separation and the death of his beloved mum together. Dom struggled very much with both of these sad experiences, however, he stayed strong and got through after some time.

To this day Dom and I are closer than ever, we love to chat, not often enough, but when we do it's always important even if it is about shit.

I have watched Dominic's daughter Bella grow over the years (via photos and stories) into the beautiful young lady she is today.

Over the years nothing has wavered, to this day I love Dominic as one of my brothers.

BARRY SANDERS
(Friend)

I first met Dom at David Lloyd in Chigwell in the mid to late 90's and on occasions he would sit and have coffee with me and some friends. What struck me most about Dom was his presence. Whilst a lot of people were intimidated by him, I saw a funny and interesting character.

In early 2010 I saw Dom several times and with the break-up of my marriage, he said "Baw, why don't you come training with me". There started our much closer friendship.

It started as training once a week, then twice and then he said "do you want to get in the ring?". So, at the age of 45 I got in the ring and got bashed up most times. Dom decided to call me "Barry the Bleed" due to me having a nose bleed on every occasion.

Six months of being bashed up by Dom, he suggested I do a white-collar fight. For a further two months five/six days a week I would be in the gym training for this fight.

Having put everything into the fight, I wanted to thank the people who had helped me which were Dom, and a couple of others. I wrote the text, sent it, read it back and thought "Oh fuck", I had forgot to put Dom's name. I immediately sent him a message saying "obviously you as well". The message I received back from Dom was "go get someone else to train you". This was a week before my fight.

I was devastated, not only had I built up this great friendship with someone who had helped me through the break-up of my marriage and got me into the best shape of my life, but I had upset him as well.

I messaged back saying can I meet him in the gym the next day, thinking I was going to get a beating off of him, but may as well get it over and done with sooner rather than later. The next day I went to the gym, shitting myself as to what the outcome would be. Dom said "Baw, I can't look at you because if I do I am going to hit you". Fortunately, he didn't look at me, I apologised and swiftly left.

The night of the fight came and we still hadn't spoken. At the end of round one, I looked down and saw Dom was in my corner. I gave it my everything for the next two rounds and after Dom came into the changing room shouting how great I had just done and it was the fight of the night.....

Another side of Dom is when me, him, Dave and all our three girls, not sure if you know this but he has a daughter..... went to Spain. We decided to go to an Italian restaurant near the apartment, but to get there you have to cross a walk way over a motorway. Dom says "I am not walking over that". We all looked at him waiting for the punch line, but oh no, this huge lump of a man is scared of heights. This man who is scared of no-one or anything is absolutely petrified. He has three young girls all taking the mickey out of him, however with the assistance of handrails and with sweat pouring off of him, a five minute walk took 20 minutes.

I think if Bella hadn't have been there he would have refused to do it for sure.

The Dom I know is not the Dom a lot of people know and see. He is a friend, part of the family. He is one of the most insecure people I have ever met and he uses his humour to hide it.

The most amazing thing is the man that has evolved over the past 25 years or so. A caring, thoughtful, loving father and the most loyal of friends.

But please never forget that there is always hidden away a man that can roar like a lion and bite like one too, but at the same time lick like a pussy cat.

I am proud to know him and call him a friend.

DAVE CANNON
(Friend)

What can I tell you about Dom?.

He is probably one of the best dads I have ever met. We all think we are great dads, he truly is. He would do anything for Bella. He sacrifices his own happiness for Bella it appears to me.

I have heard lots of things about Dom, about his past, the things he has done, what he has got up to. He has even told me stories himself, obviously never mentions any names, bless him.

Some of it sounds funny, some truly horrible but the reality of it is I can only tell you what I know. He is a lovely bloke. Have never met anyone more loyal in my life.

He would do anything for you as a mate. Would stand next to you at the gates of hell, I am sure he would. He is that type of bloke. Honestly a top top fella.

I think that some people want to be around him because of the things he has done in his past. However, from what I can work out and from what he has said, he would run away from and lose that past a quick as he could.

He has said to me on numerous times it takes you x amount of time to build up a reputation and you will never, ever lose that. I honestly think he wishes he could. But hey.

He is a genuinely genuinely lovely fella. Has always been there for me if I needed him.

We have had load of sleepovers with me, him and the girls watching stupid movies and laughing and joking about. On more than one occasion he has said to me that Bella is the only thing that has kept him alive, and you know what, I truly believe it.

I can't tell you that he is this hardened criminal who has done all these awful things, which I am sure he has. Everybody says he has done some pretty horrible stuff, but, I have never seen it.

Can't tell you anything horrible only that he is a lovely lovely bloke.

BROTHERS IN ARMS

"Family ain't always blood"

BIG JOHN
(Close Protection Security)

I couldn't ask for a better mate or better work mate as well. He has been brilliant over the last 30 years that we have known each other.

In the late 1990's we started doing the doors together, which then became licensed. The doors and the wages were half of what they had been 10 years before so we used to get these new doormen that were licensed, they weren't old school like we was.

When we started in the 80's we were a group of people and each trusted each other with their own life and obviously we all went to the gym in them days. We had all done a bit of boxing.

Nowadays all they got to do is a two-day course, phone up an agency and get sent on a job doing the door, not even knowing what they look like. You know so that side of it is lost a bit.

When we obviously got offered the work it was clean up jobs. It was go straight in and get busy. It actually worked because we didn't go back to that place again. We used to do alright and have a bit of fun. Dom was good at just whacking them.

The problem was the new ones, they couldn't get rid of the trouble basically. We got asked to take over a door in North West London, it was also a music venue but at the weekends they had club nights there. Myself and Dom went down to have a look at it. There were queues outside, people with bottles, people with drink, people fighting, and we thought we are going to have to sort this out somehow.

What we done, we put our door staff in there – but we worked the line, covering it. What we would do we'd get into the queue and look for people that was rowdy, like little groups of people and then we'd go up and attitude test them, like give them a little dig to see how they would respond. And the response was, especially if there was a group of six of them, they'd start laughing at us, but they weren't laughing after five seconds later when Dom had knocked two of them out and they were laying on the floor. I would have a little dig myself.

Within a couple of weeks we had people queuing up properly outside. Mouths closed, no drink, like proper gentlemen. Basically, what we had to do was get rid of the shit in the area and start again, that job got done.

Another time I went up to Liverpool for an event for the Millenium, it was the biggest event in Europe where they had put a marquee up, for 20,000 people. I was staying there for a few weeks.

On the actual night they asked Dom and one of his mates Big Teddy, to come down and do a bit of covert security work to see what was going on.

I was working at the front door of the place when suddenly I was getting people turn up, groups of girls and couples with fake tickets. I just said to them to "wait there and I will see what I can sort out". So basically, I got Dom to come to the front door, I explained the situation to him and said "It's not on" and that the girls are here crying, they had spent all their money and the Millennium was a one-off night and that.

We said we will go out and have a look and see what's going on. So, the three of us went out and a few people came with us with their dodgy tickets and showed us who was selling them.

There was a group of them, just next to a wall, just along from the Liver buildings. So, I said come on let's go get stuck in. Dom's gone whack, he has whacked one and there was a little wall about two foot high and this bloke has gone sliding back over the wall. What we didn't realise at the time is that there was a 12ft drop on the other side.

Dom's whacked one and got him in a headlock. I've whacked another and got him in a headlock and we looked over the wall and said to the bloke, "oi get back here" and he got back up and we said "right, see all these people here you just robbed them – get your money out your pockets". He emptied all the money out and we made him give the money back to them all.

They still couldn't get into the venue because they didn't have genuine tickets but at least they got a bit of entertainment for the night (laughs and their money back. They were loving it.

Me and Dom got a bit of a reputation to do things, that's really when the clean-up jobs started. What it was, was like I said earlier, the doormen weren't the sort of doormen from years before and because we had a bit or form we had no chance of getting a licence.

We got offered a club in Bedfordshire. They were getting a ton load of aggro up there. Me, Dom and Big Teddy, the three of us went up there. It was very easy to see who were the troublemakers as soon as you walked in. There was two groups of them. So, we walked in, walked up to them and said "get out", with the usual response from the groups – laughing. Whack! Dom's gone whack whack whack to three of them, they are down. I've whacked one, Teddy's whacked one, and with that we have gone.

I was speaking to someone from the local area who obviously didn't know it was me who had gone up there and says "it all went wobbly. Apparently, a big firm came down from London, about 20 of 'em and said they were speaking to the barmaid and there were seven people laying unconscious on the floor at one time. She'd been told there must have been about 20 of them, cos people ain't gonna believe that seven people knocked unconscious by only three people, especially when the two groups were about 12/13 people.

That was the sort of things we did anyway, the clean ups.

I have known Dom for many many years. Every Xmas week me, Dom and a few friends always used to meet up. This was about 13/14 years ago, we met up about 6pm for a meal, started getting on the red wine. It was a friend of ours restaurant and they shut at midnight.

By that time, we had had a few drinks and decided to go somewhere else. Normally we get respect from any doormen, they know us, we had probably worked with a lot them. But this place we had gone to, it was a load of new doormen, they were all Eastern Europeans. This place didn't shut till 2am and it was just after 12. We walked up and the guy said "NO". Dom was like "What mate? No what?". As Dom had said that the doorman pushed him.

Well, as soon as the doorman has pushed him I've gone boom to the one next to him. I've laid him out and gone into the place. Dom has laid the other one out. As I've gone into the bar, you can see upstairs two other doormen running down towards me. One big muscle, was looking at what was happening at the door as I come in, so I've whacked him as he was running to it. He has gone straight out and Dom has come through and done the other one.

Obviously when we do something like this we try to get away as quick as we can. Dom has turned around to go and as he has done that, I see out of the corner of my eye another two running towards us from the back. I've gone "Dom, we ain't finished yet". He has turned around and we have gone Bang and we done them. Laid them out.

It goes against what we preach when we were on the doors but it's that they didn't know us and we do like to have a bit of respect.

Dom the next day got a phone call from the doormen saying "we are really sorry, we were messing with the wrong people". He was like "that's ok, we shouldn't have been doing what we did. However, we ended up going down there and having a drink with them". I think a couple of them might have done work with us after that. One way of getting to meet people.

Things have changed now. We have moved away from that now obviously. I am on my own with my kids and Dom has Bella. We do the best we can for our children. We do it with pride, the way it should be done.

I miss the old days, I miss not seeing Dom as often.

GARY BEDFORD
(Friend)

I have known Dom since he was around 10 years of age.
He was a little chubby kid who wore round glasses. He
was always playing up and down the road with his radio-
controlled cars. Even then he was cheeky, but a nice
grounded kid. He loved his mum like a son should and still
gets very emotional when talking about her (RIP Stella).

Who would think that this little kid would turn out to be
a great athlete, a very talented boxer who went under the
name of "The Milky Bar Kid", reference to the curly haired,
glasses wearing kid in the advert.

I had the pleasure of being his trainer and cornering him
for 22 of his fights of which bonded us even more as I got
to see the real Dom.

He has a heart of gold if he likes you. If he doesn't, he'll
let you know. He doesn't suffer fools easily. He is a very
funny guy with a somewhat sick sense of humour. He says
it how it is. He is a big child at heart.

A softness runs through his veins. He loves his music and
when he listens to meaningful lyrics' he gets very
emotional. He is incredibly generous, especially to Belles!
his daughter, she is his life.

He is very insecure, feeling that he hasn't achieved and
always beating himself up that he may have let someone
close to him down.
He is too loyal for his own good.

Back in the day he always felt he had to sort people's
problems out, especially when someone took a liberty. He
needed to let people know who Dominic Negus was, when
most people knew not to cross him anyhow.

Although Dom has humbled so much in these later years,
he is someone who even now won't back down, especially
if he feels he is right.

A guy took a liberty whilst driving years ago and tried to
intimidate Dom. When Dom got out the car, the guy
obviously had second thoughts. Locking his car door.
Dom put his fist through the guy's window and tried
pulling him out of the car.

MICKY THEO
(Friend)

Me and Dominic go back years, probably from Champions Gym in Walthamstow. We used to train up there every now and then and he would come and see us.

We weren't that close in those times, we got closer down the line and ended up meeting Sundays for a coffee and a catch up on what was going on in our worlds and still do to this day.

There are no funny stories but he is a funny guy, that I can say. He cracks me up, he makes me laugh. He takes life a little bit too seriously sometimes and sometimes I sit down and talk with him and put him on the right road, otherwise he would be going off the road a lot of the time.

He is a caring person, one that is always by your side and just a great guy.

LEE MATTHEWS
(Sunday Breakfast Partner)

I knew of Dominic from when I was younger. I had never met him personally up until about five years ago. What was strange was everyone he knew from his younger days and everyone I knew from my younger days were the same people, but we were never in the same company at the same time.

I knew of him from his boxing career and as I said I met him five years ago in a café/deli and it has gone on from there really. It was first just walking in and saying "hello" and before long we were sitting on the same table and we realised we both knew the same friends. As I said it just snowballed from there. But I just clicked with Dom. The first time I sat with him at the table I just got him. I got that he is a very loyal heartfelt person.

I have been through some bad patches myself with my private life and he has always been there for me for someone to talk to and he has always listened. He is just a great character all round in my book.

We just have fun. We are busy in our daily lives and when we meet on a Sunday it is just a release. We talk about sport, boxing. We all love our boxing. We all love the trojan gladiator sport. We all like to think we are gladiators in some sort of shape.

We have a laugh and joke and I come away feeling refreshed. If I don't go and don't see Dom I kind of feel like I have missed out.

I would like to turn around and say he has done something horrible to me, so you can have something nice and horrid, but he has only ever ever been a stand-up loyal person to me. I can only give him credit all the way through. He is a 10 out of 10.

I have got so many different names given to me by Dominic to be fair – he loves a nickname. James Coburn is his favourite he says I remind him of him. There is a story to go with it. Once I got to know Dom really well and we clicked. Something was on his mind and he texted me to say "are you coming and meeting me for breakfast on Sunday?" I was like yeah. He was like "great, can't wait". When I got there, he was all happy and all smiles, like he normally is. We always greet each other with a big manly hug. He said "I know what it is with you now, you remind me of someone". I was "OK, who?" A lot of people say I look like Lee Evans to be fair and I thought he was going to come to out with that but he said "James Coburn" and started laughing. Later that day he sent me a picture of him with a funny hand and it has stuck with him and that's what he calls me all the time.

Another name he calls me is Mr Perfect. Apparently, he thinks I am perfect all the way round!!

He really is a big soft grizzly bear. He is good hearted. He is very loyal. What I like about him is you know where you stand with him. That's the sort of way I have been brought up. We tell the truth. Sometimes we can have a discussion and differ on our opinions. I am not one to agree just to agree with someone and I think he likes that. I tell him the truth.

He must like me because sometimes I nick a bit of food off his plate. He gives me the deadly face and then laughs after. If I took a hash brown he would go "oi", then laugh and say "help yourself".

I have the utmost respect for him and I hope I have many more years of his company.

TERRY HILL
(Friend)

How I met Dominic. Everyone knows who Dominic is. He is quite infamous around Essex, East London and things like that.

Me and Terry Stone, who is a well know known actor and club promoter who started Garage Nation, One Nation. We were going to watch Connor Benn at the 02 it was 2017/2018. Connor had been in one of Terrys film, the Rise of the Foot Soldier and had played his dad. We were invited to go to the 02 in a box at the early stages of his career, before he got the mega super status he has now. He was second on the card.

As we walked into the box Dominic was doing the security. He saw me and Tel walk in and was straight over on us like "hello boys, how are ya?" and we just hit it off, just like that. Dom was working and doing the security but he sat with us watching the fight, and we had a great night. Nigel Benn was there too. We just became friends after that.

Every Thursday I would get a phone call from him saying "you alright? Do you need anything? How's it going?" He did that constantly for about a year. Just every Thursday checking in to make sure I was ok. Through that we became friends. He calls me the young Burt Reynolds.

Now we are at the point where he will come round my house, you know everyone portrays Dominic as this big hard man, but they don't see the side where he is sat on my sofa playing with my kids. He comes round for dinner, you know what I mean.

His heart has overtook his reputation. Its bigger, you know what I mean he is just a nice bloke. If you are lucky enough to be in that close circle of Dominic and know the real Dominic, you will know he has a heart of gold and will do anything for you.

Obviously, we know he has got his reputation, no doubt about it. That fire still burns inside. But the side I see where he is sat on my sofa, letting my daughter put stickers all over him, or going out for Sunday lunch with him and his daughter, that's a side a lot of people don't see of Dominic. We have become really close over the years. I class Dominic as one of my best friends now.

Later in his life, he is kicking on a bit now lol.

If I don't speak to Dominic once in a week, I get a call from him "is everything ok mate, is everything ok?". He checks in with ya, just there for you if you need him and vice versa basically. Every now and then you will get a call saying "I haven't seen you for ages, I miss you. Let's go for dinner with the kids". Bella will come too. We have had loads of nights out, but he doesn't drink now, so we now just go for a Sunday Lunch or dinner with the kids. One of his favourite little haunts is the Blue Boar. Now Bella works there though. I remember when she first started working there and he was like "you going down there for dinner" I was like yeah. He said "I'm gonna skip out this week, cos Bella is starting there, but you make sure no cunt talks badly to her". That fire is still in his belly, it's definitely still there, if the wrong buttons pushed.

As much as he has this big reputation as this hard man and all that, there is a big heart. There is a side to Dominic that people don't see. He is a big softie really. He is very sensitive. He is an over thinker and his heart is in the right place. As I said his heart has overtaken his reputation. Its bigger than his reputation now.

I have been around his house and all his Star Wars toys that he collects are all out. He has got a soft, dopey side to him as well. He has matured and mellowed out with age.

He is very thoughtful, as I said if he hasn't heard from you he always calls or texts to see if you are alright, even though he might be dealing with his own demons at the time and I think he has a lot of his own demons.

He is Dominic and I think his reputation will always be there but he really is a loveable rogue.

RICKY GROVER
(Actor and Comedian)

Before I met Dom, someone said to me who I know "oh
he's a bully" and I thought I wasn't gonna like this geezer,
I'm not going to like him. I know he is a big lump but I
have heard through the grapevine he can have a row and
bang a few people over.

However as soon as I met him, I instantly liked him. I
first met Dom through boxing, it was at a boxing show.
Someone said "That's Dominic". He was shouting things
over to me because of bits and pieces that I had done that
he knew about.

He was very loud, very loud, big jokes, in your face, big
laughs and I can understand when I say a normal punter, a
normal punter is someone who we may call from the fight
world is a normal average person, might think he is a thug
or a bully. But what I really believe about Dom and I sussed
it out immediately, because where I am from you have to
weigh up people and situations very quickly, and that is
Dominic Negus is actually quite shy.

You talk to him about something that's got a bit meaning
to it, like recently we found out our friend is unwell, is very
ill or you talk to him about something that has happened
to a kid or you talk about his daughter or anything like that
he wells up pretty quickly. He is quite an emotional
person.

I suffered a lot of abuse and that as a kid. My step father
was an armed robber, there was always guns in my house.
I was brought up in a place with gangsters about and you
never knew when it was or wasn't gonna go off. I don't
know about his childhood, where he is from and what he
has been through. You will generally find that every
fighter has a story. I think I remember he was bullied at
school, blond, skinny, glasses, nicknamed the milky bar kid
and I would imagine where all this comes from, so you
know it's like the worm that turned. The one that was
being picked on and bullied, all of a sudden, he grew into
this man mountain, as strong as a lion, punch holes in
walls. He has come from a world where he got mixed up

in things he shouldn't have got mixed up in, which he will be the first to say.

Dom is a fighter but also very emotional person. What happens with people like that, I know, I am one me self is that there is no middle ground. You are either cuddling someone or you are strangling someone. You either wanna kill 'em or love 'em. Sometimes we get it wrong, we go mad at someone and if they look frightened, we go the other way and be over bloody caring.

As being a boxer, I know this book isn't wholly about boxing, but I will say the weight divisions are there for a reason. When you go to the heavyweight division, which Dom is now, he's a bit like myself, can put on a bit of suet very quickly. When you are a heavyweight fighter it is almost a different sport, when you step into that ring, forget sport, forget boxing, you are putting your life on the line.

It's not like two blokes fighting at 10/11 stone, when you get two 19 stone blokes or more smashing into each other. I will give you an idea. The average person on the street, if they chinned them full pelt, they would either kill them or very best they would end up in a coma.

People don't realise but you find all the really good heavyweight fighters are a little bit crazy, because you have to be. And Dom has got that bit of crackers, he has got it in a nice way though.

I think there's something in all of us that is fascinated with fighting. No one wants to see a one-sided fight, where someone gets bullied and gets a good hiding. When you get two big ones really having it and Dom would be one of them people, go up against each other, I think even the staunchest vegetarian in their electric car would stop and watch. There is something in all of us, maybe it's a primal thing or something, that when there is fight and you never know what the outcome is gonna be, you are going to watch it.

Also, I think it is very much a British culture thing. We love an underdog, we always have. Where the Americans love a winner, we always want the underdog to win. I think coming from where we come from that's how we feel, we are fighting against it.

In recent years you see people like Tyson Fury who is somewhat big get in the ring with someone with massive muscles and smoking tattoos and you would think he has no chance, but because he is a fighter at heart, he wins through, comes through.

I have gone full circle, but if I was to sum Dom up he is a fighter with a lot of layers. I find Dom very funny and endearing. He has a very nice way about him. He has got really good manners. You often find with fighters they have really nice manners, they have respect for people.

I will say it again about Dom, you should never judge a book by its cover.

Dom and I have a connection, not because we are fighters but because I know where he is coming from and what he is about. We got on straight away from when we first met and I think we will always get on. As I said I immediately liked him and I'm not a bad judge of character because of the sort of thing I have been through.

Dom is the real deal. I just think he is just a nice fella, but a fighter and always will be. There is a lot of people out there who talk a good fight, and a lot of the youngsters today that stick things into each other, stab each other. Anyone from my world sees that as cowardly behaviour. Dom is the person who would hold his hands up and let's have it, but not many people would do that with him. Only when he had the attack and they used weapons and stuff.

The most powerful part of Dom is his sensitive side, not the growler. You don't have to put a front up of how tough you are. I think though he is learning that. I think it is happening naturally anyway.

He will always have that part, you know that mental part, I think that is more powerful than his big punch.

ADAM WOLF
(Friend)

I have known Dominic since I was a kid really. We met at a boxing gym. I always looked up to him as a big powerful bloke and decent fighter. A lot of people respected him, not just in the boxing, just as person.

There is definitely an element of fear people have with him but it is more respect and admiration for what he was doing. He was a proper athlete, a warrior really.

He used to train his arse off and when I started getting into the amateur boxing when I was in my late teens, a young adult, I would train with him at the Lloyd twice a day on and off in between fights he had and I had. We would help each other out, moving around, sparring.

Being around the boxing we met lots of people. He wasn't my trainer effectively, but in a roundabout way he was. We trained so much together. When we weren't in the boxing gym we would whether it would be down Harold Hill or Sparta, we would train together, regularly. We would go running, tons of CV.

I am 39 now, Dom is about 12 years older than me. When I was knocking around with him I got introduced to lots of people. Dom always had loads of people wrapped around him, some for the right reason and some for the wrong reasons. Lots of hangers on, a lot of users, all that sort of stuff. Some obviously really good people as well. Less than a handful, but I still talk to those people now, still have a great relationship with them now.

Moving on, just like Dom has, you get rid of the dead wood and you find out that there are so many dogs and slags out there.

There was a funny thing when I was younger. We were down the gym once. Naturally being a young lad, I had me head up me arse, he would get me up at silly o'clock, running, training, rowing, on the bag, whatever, it was nutty. It helped me and brought me along. I didn't bring me trainers one day and he said "Wolfie, open me bag, there's some money in there, go and get yourself some trainers from the gym shop".

My family never had much growing up, we never wanted for anything but that was how it was. I have opened this bag up and there was bundles of rolled up notes in this bag. I was like "fucking hell I have never seen anything like this". I was about 17/18. I took a wedge of money and went and got a nutty pair of Nike Max Air, top notch trainers. Me nor my family would never have been able to have afford a pair like them back then. I have come back with these flash trainers on and Dom has gone "You cunt, fucking hell, like how much where they?". Haha. I didn't think I was taking the piss or anything, to me I thought there was a load in the bag. I thought a couple of hundred pounds on a pair of trainers weren't gonna make a dent in it. He saw the funny side. He is good like that is Dom.

I would like to reiterate, our pasts are our pasts. We are now family men and it is important to keep my past where it is. My priority like Dom is my family and child. I am not interested in the past, I have seen what it does, I have paid the price.

I have seen people slip in and out of their pasts, it is not for me. I have seen the other side. It all seems like champagne and whiskey bottles, but it aint.

We went on a few holidays to Spain, Tenerife and in the UK. We trained and did a lot of drinking and enjoying ourselves. There was other stuff that went on as well, but I am not too interested in that. I was all about the training and enjoying ourselves.

I have always looked up to Dom, like a big brother. I have always had respect for him. As I said before, there were always people hanging around him. I can see the falseness in people that wanted to be around him because he was a big powerful bloke.

Naturally people are fearful because he was a handful, he is a big athletic man that they say has a ferocious temper and that is sadly why he got used because of his presence, because of his temper and because he wears his heart on his sleeve.

I will be honest, now that I am older and looking at it, I don't feel sorry for him, because it's nothing like that, it is just a shame you can see it for what it is. It takes away the

51

glamour/kudos, it sort of spoils it a little bit. It's not that he was my childhood hero, but you know someone you look up to and respect and then you see it for what it really is. The nitty gritty, the dogness of people and how slaggy people can be and use each other.

To be fair, I have learnt myself from his mistakes as well, probably not as quickly as I should of done. I went down a wrong path and made some wrong decisions myself. But I am the sort of person, like Dom, that was the only way I would ever have learnt.

I speak to Dom still regularly, we chat. We get each other. We don't see each other as often as we should, but we all have busy lives now. We work hard, and we are family orientated. I know he is. He loves Bella to bits.

He really is like a big brother.

I will tell you this one funny story, I don't want to make Dom look bad, but it is quite funny. There was this geezer taking the piss. He was a Z list celebrity. He was on the step machine. Dom was always polite, but people would always try and push the boundaries and when they do, they don't like the result. I am a little bit similar, I am very very patient, but I get to a point where my patience wears thin, and I can lose me rag. Anyway, Dom asked the guy how long more he had on the machine and he was like "two minutes". So, Dom being respectful gives it five or six minutes, and goes back round and the guy was like "yeah, yeah," giving him the sort of fuck off feels, and then said "another five minutes or so". This happened a couple more times. I then see Dom scratching his head, getting the hump and then he just grabs hold of him and strangled him with his earphones and the geezer was like "ahh", trying to keep up on the treader whilst getting strangled. It was hilarious.

The mad thing is after Dom drives himself mad after about what he has done. Even though the guy took the piss and pressed his buttons and really tried mugging Dom off. He had provoked the situation and then Dom feels bad about reacting like that. But it was fucking hilarious. I thought it was funny and great. I was like "It's fine Dom, the guy took the piss".

If I thought he was wrong I would tell him as well. We have that sort of relationship. Trust me though, I wouldn't want to fall out with him. We have never fallen out, but he has been angry with me a few times. He has threatened to take my head off once or twice. But that's what happens, when you are tight with someone. And believe me I could be a cheeky little fucker when I was younger.

There are a few more stories like that, when we have been away, had a little rough and tumble but as I said I don't want to go into the stories about that.

People don't really understand Dom, and that is the trouble. They make an opinion, people judge people by what they were, what they hear, what they see, without actually sitting down and talking to that someone. I think he is misunderstood. I think with Dom there is a lot going on underneath. He has got a big smiley face and it's like "Big Dom, Big Dom" and all this but really he is just like anybody else. We are all humans. But he is dangerous, there is no doubt about that. I think that's what makes it worse, because he is quite emotional and he wears his heart on his sleeve. When he does feel that he has been taken the piss out of, it really does hurt him.

He is a warrior, he is a fighter. He loves fighting. I think he would have been perfect 200 years ago when you used to have to go into battle, wading in with axes and swords. I would want him on my side.

If he can help someone he will. He works really hard doing 2 or three jobs. The people he works with most aren't right in the head and they like to push his buttons. He recently called me and said "Wolfie, I feel like fucking killing this geezer", it's like a hammer wanting to smash an egg, and he feels guilty having these thoughts after.

He knows he could go back to his previous life and earn a fortune, but he really is not interested. As tough and frustrating as his job now is, he just wants to go to work, earn an honest living, have his family and be happy and that is it. I think anyone that doesn't admire that more than being a face, there is something wrong with them or watch too many films.

Let us all just be happy and well with our families.

PAUL (Para Paul) ATLEE
(Friend)

I first met Dom around 1998 when I was working behind the bar at David Lloyd in Chigwell. Dom used to come down there all the time. He was friends with some of the personal trainers, Lee Ottey, Wayne Cummings are a couple of the names I remember. Dom was always there and being a loud, larger than life character, we got talking and just clicked.

I was only 18 at the time, a young skinny kid. He made a beeline for me and we started our friendship from there.

I remember one of our first meetings, he kind of got me into trouble. He always liked messing about, and he came behind the bar and picked me up and started wrestling with me. He put me on top of the bar and started pushing me playfully about. I couldn't do anything, he was a heavyweight boxer at the time. Anyway, the manager called me in and I got into trouble for fighting with a member. I was like "what did you want me to do, he literally had come round and threw me on the bar". It was all in jest anyway, it was Dom mucking about. I had no control about what was going on.

He was at the height of his boxing career then and loads of us from the David Lloyd used to travel around to watch all of his fights.

As I said, we just hit it off. We would always go out, Blue Mondays, Faces and loads of the local haunts.

I was kind of in awe of him, as I said I was 18 at the time and Dom was 10 years older than me. I always remember looking up to him and thinking I would love to be like you when I grow up, that type of thing. Everyone knew him, everyone respected him. I just liked him a lot.

When I left the Lloyd I went off and joined the Parachute Regiment. In Dom's first book, he made a reference to me at the back saying "Paul, one of our true fighters for our country. You are a true man and a nice guy". I kept in touch with him throughout my Army career even though we didn't see much of each other as I was doing tours abroad.

For his Audley Harrison fight I brought a few of the guys from Colchester base down to Wembley to shout and support him.

After my career in the Paras, I had bulked up a bit and was no longer the young skinny kid that he first met. We would travel around and work security at boxing events. We did one in particular, Amir Khan vs Graham Earl at the Bolton Arena 2007. Khan won the fight, but it kicked off in the crowd, there were chairs being ripped up and thrown I think a few people were hurt quite bad. Me and Dom managed to grab a few of the perpetrators and 'kindly' escorted them out the back fire exits. Afterwards we were invited to Khans afterparty, which was also his 21st Birthday.

There was a big screen showing Hatton vs Mayweather, loads of free drinks and food. We had a fun 'after after' party back at our hotel room as well. Happy days and happy times!

We had a big night out in Brighton, there was about 10 of us that went. From the off, apart from the driver, everyone was getting drunk in the car. We were doing God knows what at the hotel. We went out for the evening and it was just carnage. We went to this bar all drinking Galliano, Dom did pretty much a whole bottle on his own, yellow bottle. Everytime I see Galliano now I always think of Dom. I think it kicked off at that bar, the bouncers didn't do anything. There was a couple of heavies with us and the bouncers just stepped back and let it all calm down until we disappeared.

We went back to the hotel after and all I remember is Wayne trying to do front flips through the hotel lobby. He landed heavy on his back and ended up slumped in a hotel lobby chair and just spewed up. Yellow puke (from all the Galliano) all down his white t-shirt. It was vile, but little things like that you don't forget.

The next day we were walking along Brighton seafront and we saw Chris Eubank. Dom said hello to him and Chris knew who he was and they had a chat. I was totally in awe that these people knew Dom. I was like "wow, this is fantastic".

He had a fight at the Country Club once. Something went on with him in the toilets and after he came up to me and said "we have to go, now". We made a very quick exit out the back door and jumped into a cab and disappeared. Not quite sure what happened in the toilet but it was a very very quick exit.

We used to go Faces a lot of the time and he used to come back and stay with me. He knew my mum, dad and brother and he used to just turn up, make a cup of tea and put his feet up. One night, I think he had had an argument with his girlfriend. He turned up and he did the most horrible fart and choked me out of the room. He was on a very high protein diet but he stunk me out me own bedroom. It was disgusting. A memory or smell I won't forget.

I was witness to a pretty big row between him and Nic. I was driving Dom and he needed to pop into his house to get something. Nic was in and it just erupted between them, not sure what triggered it but I was waiting outside the house and just hearing this screaming and yelling. At one point I heard Nic say 'so what you gonna do then - chin me?! And Dom replied 'yeah, which one?'. I was just thinking for fuck sake, get out of there before something stupid happens. Just then he came bursting out through the front door all red faced shouting all sorts of fuck offs.

He jumped into my car and we headed for my house. Driving down the main road, just before we turned into my cul-de-sac, we saw Nic come flying down the road from the opposite direction, she pulled in front of me and jumped out the car. Dom jumped out from my car now the pair of them are having a stand-up slanging match right in the middle of the main road. Our cars are blocking both directions and traffic is now building up. I went over to Nic's car, Bella was in there! I grabbed Bella and took her into my house. I went back to try and get Dom.

I noticed some people were getting out their cars to see what the hold-up was. When they saw a fully enraged Dom in the middle of the road they chose to return to their cars and not get involved! Probably a wise move!

I'm not good with smells (like the bit when he choked me out of my bedroom). There was another occasion when I was driving him back from one of our early morning training sessions at Krunch gym in Waltham Abbey, we had a two year old Bella in the car with us and I thought I could smell something! Dom said it wasn't him, he then looked in Bella's behind and then said 'yeah there's a few little nuggets down here!". I started retching straight away. He then put his hand down there and picked them out and threw them out the window. My head was out the window at this point trying not to throw up in my car! Sorry Bella!

What I really want to get across is there are probably a lot more people that know Dom's more vicious side to him and want to talk about all the fights and all that sort of stuff. I want to get across that he has such a soft side to him. He is just a proper, nice, reliable guy. I have so much time for him and I have always respected and looked up to him.

When my brother tragically passed away in 2006, he came around and spent a week with me, supported me, just there for me. He was a rock of support for me at that time and I am eternally grateful for that.

If he is on your side you cannot wish for a nicer person to have, but if you get on the wrong side of him, get your running shoes on.

I am proud to call him my friend.

JASON BURTON - BURTY
(School Friend)

I have literally grown up with Dom. I met him at Junior School, we must have been about eight. We used to muck about at school and then spend most of our time out and about after school playing on our bikes. Cyril and Stella were like second parents to me and I was often having dinner round there. I used to live two roads down from

57

him. There was a handful of us knocking around together, messing about, just little bits of mischief.

Once school broke out if my mum and dad weren't home, I would go round to his. Once my homework was done, I would be straight round at Dom's. His home was like my second home. I spent so much time round there as ya do when your mates are so close.

As we got older, I would say about 14, Dom would come round to mine and do some sparring in my garden with me and my dad. Gary Bedford moved in next door to me. Dom then got more involved in the boxing. I think Dom got into the boxing as he loved the sport so much.

When we were 17/18 we both had motor bikes. I was leaving Dom's house one day and Dom set Rocky the Labrador on me. Motorbikes were not that fast in those days and Rocky literally came running down the street after me. Grabbed my jeans and dragged me off my motorbike. Dom then had to chase after Rocky to get him to get off of me. It wasn't funny at the time but looking back I do laugh.

When we were a little bit older, we started doing cars up. I had an MK2 escort van but we was doing up a Austin A40 for Saloon Stocks car racing in Dom's front garden. Cyril was helping us. I accidentally cracked one of the petrol pipes without realising. I started the car up and was revving the nuts out of it and I thought it had started raining but I was being doused in petrol. Dom and Cyril did the worse thing possible and started throwing buckets of water over me. Luckily it didn't go up.

During those years Dom was like anything for a laugh. He used to like messing about and joking around. He used to love to read the boxing magazines. He was really getting into boxing. I joined a club at an earlier age, but got my nose broken and thought it wasn't for me back then.

Dom's first job was a panel beater. He used to repair bits on my car. Everyone used to help each other out. If we could we would bend over backwards for and help one another.

We were always in contact as we got older. Would go to the White Hart or the George in South Woodford for a few beers, then go on for an Indian. After a few beers, that's when the fights would happen. I was probably involved in most of them. Later we would venture to the Tottenham area, a few beers, clubbing, a few fights as you do at that age.

There was once a time in Chingford, we were at a pub talking to some young ladies. These guys came over saying the girls were with them, they were their boyfriends. No altercation happened and we left, but they came out after us. A little bit of a fight went on outside further down the road. The police sirens could be heard so we decided to do the off. We had to run through the Council depot, over the fence, across the grounds and out the other side as quick as we could.

In my eyes Dom has and always will be a gentle giant.

When it comes to family and stuff like that he is very family orientated, and when he needed to do what he needed to do he always came back to his normal self. Not like a Jekyll and Hyde, but when he needs to sort out problems, he sorts them out and when he is with family, it is just about family and helping out friends.

He is a very good friend. Even if we don't speak for weeks as soon as we are in contact it is like time has never passed, as if we had spoken that morning. That goes for the all of us. We haven't always got to be in each other's pockets, but we know we are always there for each other. A true friend.

Dom is a blinding dad. He can't do enough for Bella.

JAY COD
(School Friend)

Dom's mum, Stella, called me Jay Cod. It was remarked upon, in a previous book, that the reason for the name 'Cod' was, because I could drink like a fish, but it actually was because of the way I could swim a length underwater and first was used when on holiday in Spain. The name just stuck after that. I do drink like a fish though...

I know Dom through Danny. I have known Danny since I was five. He went to the same senior school with 'them'. Even though I went to a different school, we all used to hang about together, after school, or in the evenings. I really got to know them from the youth club. That's where I first saw Dom. He always seemed very demure and insular. I didn't really know him. Down the youthy Dom might look down in the dumps and I would be like "alright mate?? What's the matter?", He would always say "alright...". It wasn't until sometime later that I knew that he knew some of the same people as I did. At the time, I was really more interested in playing badminton.

From my recollection of knowing Dom, I heard that he was bullied in his early teens. To the stage that Dom didn't want to go to school anymore. He is the classic case of the worm that turned.

The people that bullied Dom became his nemesis and the people that treated him with respect and compassion, became his friends. He has got great loyalty with regards to that. You become family. You earn that trust. It takes a while, but there is this really strong bond.

Dom grew big and strong. And anyone that thought they could still bully him, if they bumped into him later on, got their comeuppance. It was not Dom getting his revenge, it was Karma. It is like, "you are not going to do this to me anymore, to bully me anymore" and was just commanding some respect. In some cases, well deserved...

As a group there was a few years between the youngest and eldest, but all our birthdays were all about the same time as each other. We were also all in bred, lol, all half cuts of some sort, mongrels. During that time, we were all skin heads or mods, you know the fashion scene. It was a difficult time to have all these different cultures, but we was fine with it. It didn't matter what religion, colour or creed you were, we didn't really care. It was great, culinary wise we all discovered each other's cuisines. I remember being around Fred's (Dom's brother) one time and having best lasagne I have ever had. We are all multi ethnic. It never entered our minds though. We were just friends, family. There was no prejudice between us. We teased amongst each other, but we owned that banter between us.

Dom was notoriously late for everything. When I used to go around to his house to meet up, I was always greeted by Cyril, Dom's dad. "Hello boy, come on in. Dom will be back soon. Do you want a cup of tea?". The hospitality was always out of this world and he always had stories to tell whilst I waited for Dom. I really enjoyed just sitting there chatting and likewise with Stella, Dom's mum. She was always offering cups of tea. I always declined and I think they thought that was strange. They both soon realised that I actually didn't drink tea .... Haha. They were just a really good family. Happy. Close knit.

If I remember correctly, one of the stories was that Dom's dad stayed behind in World War 2 after the landings at Dunkirk. He volunteered to stay and help the injured. This is the mentality Dom has got from his British side. Dom is very proud to be British and also very proud to be Italian.

Reflecting on an incident in a restaurant, that has been referred to by others. My recollection of it was, it was just myself and Dom there to start with. There wasn't an altercation, but there was some real animosity from these three big guys that had come in. Using derogatory language. I believe one of the references being made to Dom was him being called Joe 90 due to his specs and stuff. This was before his eye laser treatment. They were pissing off the other diners too and being aggressive towards the staff.

I remember Dom getting really riled up about it and I was like "just ignore them, don't worry about it". Anyway, Dom got up I thought he had gone to the bathroom, but he had gone and made a phone call and he came back and said "it is sorted".

We continued to wait for our main course. Some other friends, in the meantime, turned up at restaurant. They sort of knew who Dom was, but were more my friends from another group if you like. I voiced my concern to them saying "maybe you should take yourselves and the girls to the back, it might get a bit nasty sitting here". They sort of laughed at me. I was seriously concerned, I remember saying, "No, you better go. Either leave the restaurant of sit well away from Dom and me". As I was having the conversation and they were moving to the back of the restaurant, Dom got up and strode across the tables. It's the only way I can explain it. He literally jumped over people's dinners.

What he had seen was Fred approaching the entrance of the restaurant, actually it was Fred's hat he saw which was the trigger, his cue, which he hadn't told me about. That was it. It all kicked off. There was an altercation. John followed Fred in and it kind of got quite heavy. Fisticuffs and what have you.

One of the guys then announced he was a policeman and that he could fight. Dom was like "well come on then". He was as large as Dom. Meanwhile I think Fred had taken a bit of a knock. They then turned their attention to John and they were trying to pull John out of the restaurant. He was hanging onto the door frame as if to say, "you are not taking me outside". I ran across and pushed one of them out of the door, this freed John to come back into the restaurant. It was at that point, which I think some have forgotten, was when the windows went through. We were inside and the two guys that were outside put the windows through. These guys were meant to be police.

All the diners and my other friends, in complete shock, had left their meals, now covered with glass and moved to the back of the restaurant, they had to run away and were now standing frozen. Nobody else got involved. The manager at this point, was on the phone to the police. There was a bit of a stand-off, but the three guys thought better of trying anything else and were looking a bit battered. I think they was very surprised, that they took a beating. The police turned up very quickly.

When the Bobbies, the uniformed police, arrived we were all told to sit down and they started taking statements, trying to get an idea what had just happened. The other three guys were arguing with the owner of the restaurant. He (the manager) pointed at us and said, "it had nothing to do with them, they hadn't done anything wrong".

With that, I think it was a sergeant as he had a few stripes on him, then announced that we should leave. The other three guys started protesting quite loudly "what you are letting them leave?? What's going on??". As we were leaving I actually heard one of the uniformed officers say to them "this is not how we expect one of ours to behave". I have no doubt that these three guys were police as I recall one of them flashing a badge at one stage. They might have been plain clothed police that had gone out for the night and thought they could intimidate someone just because they were wearing glasses.

We all just walked out, I think I paid the bill, I knew the owner. We were all barred after. The owner said to me "I would appreciate if you wouldn't come back to the establishment". It was about two years later I went back with another friend and they turned and said "we don't serve this person". So, they did remember. I acknowledge that was fair for us to have all been barred.

I remember he did point out to the uniformed police that it wasn't our fault. We also didn't smash anything. We didn't smash the windows, they did. They were obviously off their rockers at the time, but they became very unstuck, they weren't particularly in very good shape afterwards. They came off worse for sure. With a couple of shiners and cut lips.

The police sided with us as the proprietor said it had nothing to do with us and they believed him. We didn't hesitate, we just left. I recall Dom and Fred might have been laughing as we left...to see the 'fuzz' being 'nicked'. I reckon that if the fight had continued, Dom could have taken all three of them on his own.

There might be some other fight stories I might reveal on my death bed, but I will never be proud of them. There was never a sense of achievement or bravado for me. All I will say is, none of them were unprovoked. I don't know why people always picked on Dom or why he managed to find these altercations, but they were certainly never started by us. They were always finished by Dom and or us as a collective. As a group that is what we were like. We were not a gang looking for trouble, but things got sorted out, if trouble found us.

With regards to Dom's debt collecting days, I actually think he was quite fair about it, he tried to resolve issues, rather than being a bull in a China shop, I'm guessing. I'm not really familiar with that part of his 'career'.

I was wary of his bouncer friends. I didn't particularly frequent in those circles because I don't belong in that environment. It is beyond my world, my understanding. That type of environment was a very different scenario.

In those dark times, when Dom went off the rails a bit and what have you, I didn't have a lot of contact with him, definitely less contact than usual, however when we did get together it went straight back to how it was with us. I think that is what Dom missed. What's not to like? All fun and no aggro.

With regards to the underworld, hardman, enforcer & "gangster" chapter of Dom's life, I don't know about that. There has been lots of turning points and realisations, that only Dom could tell you what they were. I don't ask him about the nitty gritty. I don't pursue him about it. He doesn't want to relive that. We are just happy he is alive and got through it. We are just happy that we can go back to how we were. The rest of us were never in that league, never in that world, never in that, different existence. And

Dominic with Bella

With Warren Barnes and 'Eggy'

With James Smith

With Lyle Gornall

Dominic (with from left) Keith Durso, Dave Gibson, Lyle Gornall, Dave Decar
and 'Henry'

With Rob Scott

With Mark Potter

Steve Head and Terry O'Neill

With Mark Potter (seated), Gary and Jim Hemmings

With Ricky Grover

With Terry Hill

With Alan Neil

With Eddie Lam

With Barry Sanders

With Lee Asher and Alan Neil

Young boxers; Dominic, Lee Butler and Mark Potter

With Jimmy Yellop

With Mike Jackson

With Alan Mortlock , Gary Bedford and Noel Tierney

Dominic (centre) with from left Freddy & Stella Negus (Dom's brother and mother), Bob Lonkhurst (British Boxing Board of Control Inspector) and Cyril Negus (Dom's father)

Dominic 'The Milky Bar Kid' Negus,
as he boxed as a professional

With from left, Craig, 'Big Chris', Liam and Connor

With former World heavyweight champion Tim Witherspoon and boxing
promotor & actor Harry Holland

With Vic Smith and Dan Barber

now Dom seems to be floating back to us, back to normality, back to reality, away from that gangster life type of thing.

Dom has gone through many changes in his life. He can be quite a complex person. Sometimes he can be very quiet, sometimes demure. He is sometimes sensitive emotionally, not like me. Sometimes Dom needs comforting. He has got vulnerabilities. The hard man exterior with a soft centre. I am particularly emotionless and thick skinned, whereas Dom can be empathetic. I think that is a better trait than what I have got, because he cares about stuff. We are actually all quite different, but we know each other's traits. And I think I speak for everyone, in this collaboration, despite our differences, we have always looked out for each other.

When Cyril, Dom's dad died his funeral was difficult. There is footage of the ceremony. I'm not suggesting that it be viewed, but it gives you an idea about how Dom copes. He was making light with everyone gathered before the ceremony, but, as soon as the funeral began that's when it really hit him. And that's when you see the change from him laughing and joking to it dawning on him and that this is actually happening. Him joking, before the ceremony, I guess was his way of coping with it and then it catching up on him and showing his sorrow and emotions. The passing of his parents was an important part of Dom's life. Sad times, even for an emotionless Cod.

We all still talk until Dom throws a hissy fit and acts like a child, haha.

Dom is a very committed person. He tells me has no desire to be a millionaire. He seems to get by with not having a lot of money. He is only interested in what he can do right now. He doesn't look beyond his capabilities, in an unrealistic or farfetched way. Of course, we all want to be rich or win the lottery, but he is firmly on the ground with regards to 'this is real, this is what I can do and this is how I am going to get my money and how I am going to live'. He has always managed and not ever been overly concerned about being wealthy or anything like that. I am sure in the past while he was doing other stuff, that might have entered his transition, but no, he is definitely not a greedy person, not unless you put a load of food in front of him. Dom is generous. But don't nick his chips...

Dom is a devoted father. I don't know Bella that well. Not out of choice. Dom kept her pretty much to himself, private. Protected. I can understand that.

Dom has always been dependable. Many a time when he's been there to protect us. He has always got your back.

Dom is formidable, a large fella. An accomplished boxer. There is always going to be people that want to test him. It doesn't matter how hard you are, there is always someone that is going to be harder. But I don't want to get into that. Dom is our friend. Our family.

He helps out at the shelter, he has asked my other half if she can help out with a guy there. With art stuff. Unfortunately, it wasn't something she could do. This is just another example of him wanting to help others.

Dom gets on with all our other halves. Mostly. Mine is Irish and she could probably kick the shit out of all of us....

I don't usually like talking about our past. Kinda tight lipped about it all. It is private. So, that's all. We have all moved on with our lives. But we are still all family.

DANNY WRIGHT
(Journalist and School Friend)

My very first memory of Dominic was outside Woodbridge High School, on St. Barnabas Road bridge. He was two years above me at school and would have been 15 or 16 at the time.

I remember his Michael Jackson 'Thriller' jacket, spectacles and curly hair. This perhaps made him a target for bullies. We spoke about something, that night. I can't remember, but I remember sensing an unusual energy that I haven't witnessed in anyone else.

Very soon after this, before he had officially left school, Dom would develop a reputation as a man not to be trifled with. I can see three reasons for this.

1. The aforementioned unusual energy, developed partly through his experiences of being bullied.

2. A 'final punch' technique which, when landed to either body or head, would end the session.

3. A complete lack of fear.

We were regulars at the White Hart pub in South Woodford, which is no longer there. After a visit there, we often used to enjoy a curry in South Woodford. There are many stories regarding curry houses.

This must have been around 1990. I would have been 18 years old. After a brief meet-up in the White Hart, we decided to head for a curry. Myself, Dominic and John (Croney) had taken our seats inside, and were waiting for Jason (Cod) to enter so we could order.

Cod was good at getting himself and others into trouble. After a few minutes, I went outside to find Cod in a confrontation with a guy in a crowd of maybe ten people. Entering the group, mainly to pull Cod away, I could not understand what they were shouting, but it ended with a guy pushing me into an alleyway and approaching me with a bottle.

I managed to turn around in the alleyway and reversed, walking backwards. The guy he continued to walk towards me with the bottle. I heard a familiar voice in my head, telling me "Throw your coat over his head".

In retrospect, I can't confirm if this was indeed a voice in my head (perhaps an echo from a previous altercation) or whether the voice was issuing live instructions. I did exactly as the voice told me, and threw my bomber jacket over the guy's head. Before I even saw the coat land, I saw his whole body move 90 degrees with the force of a punch to his (covered) head.

Looking down, I could see he was unconscious, but breathing. Looking up, I saw the group he was with had dispersed very quickly towards the train station, leaving the guy lying outside Woolworths.

I heard the voice again "Too fucking risky going back in there. I'm starving, let's get a pizza." We strolled up to Pizza Hut, I recall it was a delivery only one with a couple of tables. From memory, we stayed for around 20 minutes.

Dominic had parked his Range Rover opposite the curry house, so we strolled back down to the car. Straight past two police vans, with two officers standing over a (still unconscious) man outside Woolworths, attempting to take his details.

There are a few tales regarding the same curry house, which eventually resulted in a lifetime ban for Cod. This was tested years after the initial ban, when I went in there for a curry with him. "We do not serve this person".

JONNO CRONEY
(School Friend)

I first met Dom at school, he was quiet. Always been a big character, but fairly quiet. He wasn't in the main crowd back in them days. He used to record and copy videos and that's how I knew him. He was always a lovely guy at school. Perhaps he changed a lot from school where when we met up again, I was about 18, I believe.

We were in the pub one day and you would bump into people you knew from school and they would comment "bloody hell you was the short dumpy kid at school with glasses" and that type of thing and he would take offence to that. He used to dread meeting old people from school days cos you knew it would end up one way.

It would end up sometimes with Dominic hitting them. Never in a bad way though because Dominic always puts a hand of friendship out and I kind of figured out about him over the years, his first receptive is to be friendly and wants to get on with people, but if people don't receive that he doesn't like that at all and it would only end up one way. He was a great character back then, just a big person, just great. Not gonna lie, very loud but we had some great laughs.

Just wouldn't want to get on the wrong side of him. I've heard the stories, read lots of stories and heard lots of things, but I don't see him in that way. I have also found with Dom if you treat him fairly, treat him nice, he is the best friend you will ever have. He always lights up a room and lights up your night as well. He is always fun, funny. He is always good company, very good company. He was never a trouble maker.

I always remember this story that shows both sides of him. We were in our early 20's. We were in Devon somewhere and we had all been out on the beer that night and we were pretty tanked up and I think me and Dom where the last to leave.

We were walking back to our digs and there was a bloke we found, literally laying on the kerb, absolutely drunk as a skunk he was. Dominic being Dominic was like we can't leave him here. I was like just leave him, leave him alone. He will sleep it off just leave him. Dominic was like no I can't leave him like this. Someone might come and knock him over or mug him, blah blah blah.

The guy was quite a big bloke. So, he convinced me to help. We both grabbed hold of this bloke who was literally unconscious. We picked him up, we sort of had an arm around him walking up the road, not really sure where to, maybe just to dump him on a bench somewhere.

Anyway, this guy has come round, well semiconsciously come round and sort of, bearing in mind I kept saying to Dom just leave it, leave him. The guy has come round, looked at Dom and said to Dom "who the f###ing hell are you?" Dom was like "who the f###ing hell you talking to" and whacked him one lol.

The guy was in a much worse state afterwards than he started. And that always struck me that was Dom all over. If he can help someone, then he will help, but if someone is rude to him, then you are in a bit of bother. He literally just turned and belted him. I could see it happening. The guy was drunk and like who are you and I knew what

69

Dom's reaction would be to it, so that always stuck in my mind to be honest.

There were lots of occasions with Dominic with lots of fighting involved and if that's what you want to hear that's fine, but for me that's not how I see him. I have never seen him as being a bad person, he is not a bad person. Sometimes when you read the books you would think he sounds like a bit of a nightmare. But I can honestly say Dominic over the years, I don't think I have ever seen him start trouble once, not once.

When he was in his prime and very well known, I didn't see so much of him then so I can't comment on them, but certainly when he was younger, up until the age of 25 he would always be the one to help and defend people as well.

Dom is just an absolute wind up. The banter is brutal. We don't see as much of each other as we should, but when we get together it's like being 15 again. He always meets the banter, he is very good at that and very very quick. He was always such a good laugh, we had such a scream. We keep up on WhatsApp and what not.

I think the last time I saw him he came up to Norfolk with us, we had a few days away. Bella came too.

Cyril, Dom's dad was such a lovely guy. Bless his soul. When we were young and would go out for a beer, it didn't matter what time we got back, we would always end up at Cyril's café. It could have been 10 O'clock, 11 O'clock or 2am in the morning Cyril would normally be up waiting. We would walk in and say "Cyril, put the kettle on mate" cup of tea, cup of coffee. They were just great times, just sitting there, he would tell us stories about the war and growing up and all that. We always ended up there. Everyone loved Cyril. He was such a lovely person. And mum, mum was lovely, extremely fiery. I guess that's where Dom got it from, because Stella was fiery, and brutal, very brutal. You could not say anything bad about them at all. They were very proud of Dom.

At one of the boxing matches, I think it was televised, and someone commented about mum, as all you could hear was her shouting and screaming lol. In the first row it was so funny.

ALAN NEILL
(School Friend)

I remember Dominic from an early age, maybe eight, nine or ten, we went to Ray Lodge Juniors and Woodbridge High School. But Dominic kept himself to himself very much from what I recall. I mean we were always the lesser kids if you know what I mean. We used to get picked on. He was a short, fat kid, with long curly hair and glasses, I think they were even national health ones.

No one knew what was going on in the background. I sort of knew he liked boxing but yeah no one really paid any attention to it. When kids come out with stuff you sort of go "yeah like whatever mate, that ain't gonna happen". I know he used to have people to his house for muck about boxing matches in the back garden. His mum was there. But at school no one would have known he would have taken it to another level.

We used to get bullied. At the high school there were two sets of gates, lower school and upper school. There would be kids waiting for you at the upper school gates to give you a dig. Kids of the likes of me and Dom. We would go out at the lower school gates to avoid a good kicking, but how things changed eh.

Through school he was pretty quiet, kept himself to himself. It wasn't until when we left school, I had seen him about a few times, but I didn't pay any attention to him and I heard he had started having boxing matches.

I had no idea he was doing what he was doing, like when he went into the security side, debt collector side or whatever a bit later on. You saw a totally different person to what he was at school, if you know what I mean. The expression the worm had turned.

It was weird I watched the documentary a few years ago, called Underground Britain, and the guy portrays Dominic as a right C##t if you know what I mean. He was going around debt collecting and threatening people and I thought bloody hell mate, what is going on there.

I also saw him on the telly when he fought Audley Harrison and I was like, bloody hell mate, a totally different person. Fair play to him.

My youngest son is like "Can I meet Dominic, he is a legend" because we watched that Danny Dyer thing and my son was like "Do you know him" I was like "yeah I went to school with him, we grew up together". He loved it when he met him it was like "wow I met Dominic Negus".

We reconnected on Facebook and Dominic was like "Alright Al, how are you? We must meet up and have dinner". Me and my girlfriend went down and met him.

He has got a big heart Dominic he would do anything for anyone you know. Like now, he is trying to do good. That's how it seems to me, that he wants to make amends from his dodgy past.

He is always like if you need anything Al, let us know, I will always sort you out, you know what I mean and things like that. He is very sincere like that.

Dom is a lovely man. We get on great and I really appreciate his friendship.

SANJAY
(Former Boxing Contender and Friend)

I knew Dom from a long time ago. I used to go back to the UK, through Ian. Ian was a good family friend of ours. He knew me from Spain and he invited me to go and visit his gym in the UK. I went there training and that was how I got to meet Dom, this is way before I decided to even turn pro.

I went to the gym, trained there then came back to Spain. Then one day I felt like making the decision to turn professional, so I gave Dom a call and said "Guv, what do you think, do you think you could put me on track to turn professional?" he was like yeah why not come over, will set up the meeting with Frank Warren and his son and Francis. Dom arranged the meeting and I flew over. That

72

is when our professional journey began together. We done our training in Spain and Dom used to come over with the other boys, the other lads that were training with us.

The majority of my training was in Spain and we would go back to the UK for the fights. Dom was living a Spanish life, he always used to like his "bom bom", that was his favourite coffee, mention that, he laughs, and a "cup of tea". We always used to have our own little jokes about tea and chocolates and biscuits. Dom always knew that I loved to eat, but when training I had to be very strict with my diet.

I was very serious on the boxing side of things. He always told me to enjoy it more and don't take it so seriously as it goes so quickly, it goes so fast. It is so true what he said.

One of my best experiences with Dom and my professional boxing career, even though I had a short career, was our fight in Delhi. We trained all of the Summer in Spain to try to acclimatise to the New Delhi weather. We used to do our sparring and go on the running tracks.

We went to Delhi it was amazing. We went Air India Dom drank all the wine on the plane, lol all the red wine that was, laughs. It was me, Dom and Lenny and it was a mad experience there. It was like being in a Bollywood film. Mad. There was about 16,000 people there at the time. It was a big stadium for me, I had never been on a stadium that big. Big platform, TV stars, Sky, Bollywood stars there. It was a really good platform to perform on. I was under the main event. It was really great and I feel very fortunate to have that experience. After the fight we went round to one of my uncles houses to have food and a party. It was unbelievable the whole experience.

Delhi was crazy, the press, the workouts, the traffic, the heat. I remember the night of the fight in the boxing arena changing room, they came to give me boxing gloves and they had bloody given me kick boxing gloves!!! I said "oh my god Dom, they haven't even got boxing gloves how am I supposed to fight?". It was all a mad experience. One that I will treasure for the rest of your life and it will never come again, never come again.

73

That really signatured my life with Dom, it meant so much to me and being a winner out there. I was an underdog at that fight, even though I'm Indian, British Indian, I was fighting one of the local guys. When I walked into the ring they booed me, but after I won they cheered me so it was mad. Such an important one, to go out there and win, I felt like I was fighting for a world title out there to be honest with ya.

We trained so hard and training for the weather and I think we flew out there a week or 10 days before the fight and basically I had to be so careful with what I ate, what I drank cos obviously it's a big climate change when you go from Europe or UK to Asia. Everything is different, the timing, the food, the water it's all different. I even had to brush my teeth with bottled water. I didn't want to get any infections, get ill, stomach cramp or anything like that. I was living a bit mad for the whole week.

My family, my brother came out. It meant so much to me. Dom enjoyed it, eating curry   I suppose it was good for Dom to view that sort of culture and experience because I am sure Dom has never seen anything like that before in his life either. It's a different world altogether. Nothing like Europe, UK, Thailand.

That was my best experience with us together.

Dom is a gentleman, he is a good hearted man and old school.

DEMI
(Friend)

I first heard about Dominic, I was about 20 years old and I joined the boxing gym in Walthamstow. It was about the year 2000 and I was with my friend Noel Tierney.

Obviously Dominic was very well known in and around East London and Essex, as he was sort of in his prime then.

He trained at that gym. I had heard of him, never seen or met him and a couple of years later Noel asked me if I wanted to do some security work at a boxing show in London.

I was like "yeah, yeah, I would love to do that" and he said it is obviously through Dominic Negus. I was like ooooh, a little bit nervous as I had heard so much about him and knew who he was.

There was an aura about him and so on the way there, Noel said to me "whatever you do don't get cheeky, don't answer back, just do as you're fucking told basically". So, I was like "yeah, yeah of course I will, absolutely".

Now I am even more nervous now, bearing in mind I must be about 22 now. I have walked into this hotel, I've seen five or six guys, they are all fucking huge. They are all in black suits. Noel introduced me and I've met Dominic Negus straight away.

I sort of knew who he was without meeting him because he was a mountain of a man and just loud. Not in a horrible way more a force to be reckoned with sort of way. So, we are all standing around and he is briefing us on what we have got to do, where we can stand and how things are going and Dominic I nickname him "Bully".

On the night he is doing his rounds, taking the piss out of everybody, only bantering and he got to me and he said something to me, I can't remember exactly what, I am 40 now, and it was nearly 20 years ago. He then said something about my mum, not like horrible, just school ground banter, and I turned around and went "ooh like yours".

I looked to Noel, he just dropped his head and I thought "fuck". I've instantly regretted everything I have just said. And thought fuck I am going to get the shit kicked out of me now. Dom just looked at me, laughed, he actually laughed and said "10 out of 10 for arsehole boy". That's all he said to me and after that we became good friends and to this day we have become really really good friends. That was the first time I ever met Dominic and that is my first encounter.

After that the lists goes on, its endless.

We were coming back from a fight show up north somewhere and I was driving and I had a 4x4 jeep at the time. Dominic was in the front, there were three guys in the back and then there was Noel Tierney in the boot, bearing in mind it was a four hour journey. It was about midnight and I said I needed to stop for some diesel so I stopped and Dominic then said to me watch this and I was like what ….

We got out the car, I literally see Dominic put his hand down the back of his trousers, rub his finger in between his arse crack, and opened the boot and rubbed his finger straight on Noel's top lip and went "Poo tash".

I have never laughed so much in my life and till this day still laugh about it. I don't know if that's a good story, or excuse the pun a shit story, but that is one of the things I will always remember him for and it was honestly one of the funniest things I have ever seen in my whole life, proper hilarious.

What I can say about him as a person, not a story, but for me Dominic has been like an older brother. I joined the boxing gym like I said and I started boxing. There was a couple of pro fighters in the gym and I asked them for help, and they were like you might as well give it up as you are not very good. A couple of people were rude about it and I remember saying to Dominic one day "will you help me?" and he "goes with what?". I said "with training as I want to fight again but I want you to train me" and he was like "yeah of course I will but you have to do what I say".

Training with Dominic every day we became closer and closer. Like I said I see him like an older brother. I won my fight and it was only because of Dominic.

If I am ever in trouble I can always pick up the phone, I can talk to him, I constantly ring him for advice on stuff. If I ever need relationship advice I phone him. He is like my agony aunt.

He is massively misunderstood. Dominic has a very big heart but because of his past he is very very misunderstood. I have known him for so long I know exactly the person he is.

The guy has a big heart but he also has a bad temper. Not sure if it's a good mix or a bad mix.

MICHAEL GILHOOLY
(Friend)

I moved to Spain in 2003/2004, I had got myself in a little bit of trouble back in Birmingham. My dad lived in a place called Denia in Spain. It is a posh little fishing village and about a 30 minute drive to Benidorm. A nice quiet little fishing port, mainly locals, not many tourists. I was about 23/24 and went with my girlfriend.

I was into boxing at the time and I was an amateur boxer. I was a decent boxer but as I said got myself into some trouble and went over to Spain, got myself a job with a company called Mountain Construction and was desperate to carry on boxing as thought I could maybe get somewhere. There were absolutely no boxers out there whatsoever. I did find one gym in a little town. It was called Europa gym but they did no boxing whatsoever which was a shame.

I used to go to there every day. It was a proper nice little gym, it had everything you needed there and you used to have to walk up some stairs to get into it as it was upstairs.

About two or three months later, one day I walked in there in the afternoon and I heard the biggest thudding sound I have ever heard in my life. Whack Whack Whack like someone was knocking the building down, but it was someone doing some boxing or pad work.

As I walked upstairs I could see into an aerobics room, there was this bloke and a guy that was holding the pads for him. I walked over to the door as they were in the middle of the room and I thought fuck he looks a bit familiar. I was trying to figure out what the accents were like. They sounded British, like London or Essex way and I just carried on looking.

I then had to rub me eyes as literally no word of a lie, the night before I had been reading one of the Hardmen books British Gangsters. I was into a bit of villain stuff and I had been reading about Kate Kray, one of the Kray twins wife and had literally been reading about this guy called Dominic Negus. I knew of his name anyway through the boxing and the fight with Audley Harrison.

I looked over and thought that surely can't be him but had another look and he popped his head up and said "all right mate, can I help ya?" I said to him "by any chance are you Dominic Negus?" and he said "yeah". I was like no way. I said "my names Michael and I'm from Birmingham, my dad lives in Denia and has been out here for a little while, I'm really into my boxing, obviously know who you are and all that and can't believe I am literally seeing you".

We started talking and really hit it off with him and his friend Nick. He wasn't a fighter or anything like that. Nick Cole, he was such a nice guy he was trying to break into acting at the time and we just all hit it off.

He said what you doing after and I said not much really. We ended up going to the Irish bar, Paddy's Bar which is not far from me dads' little gaff. We went and had a couple of drinks in there and just started to talk, exchanged numbers, back in the day when we didn't have smart phones or anything like that 2003.

We arranged to meet up later in the night and went to Paddy's Bar again and literally every day for the next two months we were together morning, noon and night.

We started training together, we had a little routine, we would train in the morning, go to Paddy's Bar in the afternoon and then meet up in the evening. He introduced me to drinking as well. We used to drink pints of wine mixed with lemonade and that is all we did every day.

It was great and I tell you what the best story about it is I went over there with me missus. I ended up losing me missus as she got fed up with me going out all the time. I ended up losing my job at constructions, but you know what, I will always say I had the best time of my life. Such a great time, it really opened my eyes to the world. We just used to talk all day about boxing and all the things he used to get up to. I just found him, no word of a lie, the nicest guy I have ever met. Couldn't do enough for you. He was absolutely brilliant and Nick as well.

Over the next year he would come back and forth. I brought him round to me dads for dinner. We used to go everywhere together. He took me to go and see one of his old boxing promoters that was in Torrevieja, I think his name was Dave. We just had a great time, a really good time. We did that for a couple of years. But then one night I did see the other side to him.

So, we always went to Paddy's Bar and got to know all the locals and there were a few locals from different countries. There was one particular guy called Jean Paul, a Dutch guy, spoke loads of languages, bit of a flash git as you'd call him and he thought he was the man about town. He was really up himself and the one night we was in the bar and Nick, Dom's mate was speaking to I think some American girls and Jean Paul walks in. He had obviously had a few drinks. He came in billy big balls yeah and was working the room, like he normally does. He started goading Nick a little bit about talking to these girls, he was trying to embarrass him in front of the girls.

I remember Dom was sat at the bar, in fact I was sitting to the right and Dom was to my left and Nick was talking to these girls and Dom said "oh leave him alone Jean Paul, just give him a break" and no word of a lie Jean Paul said something to Dom almost confrontational and he started walking round the bar and I thought what is he doing?

Anyway, he has walked round and Dom as quick as a flash, jumps up off his stool and honestly, he head butted him. I had to turn my face. I have never seen anything like it, it made me wince. I've been involved in loads of fights and seen loads of fights, but I have never seen anything that has made me wince like that yeah.

He head butted him that hard that the guy was out no word of a lie, a sack of spuds he went down and was out for about 20 minutes on the floor. Dom was like "oh, oh well you know", but I was like, "Dom", and he said "but I didn't know what the guy was gonna pull out". I thought the guy must have had a death wish to confront Dom. But I still wasn't ready for what I saw that night. He headbutted him and he has gone flat to the ground.

By the time he has come round the lump on his head is bigger than his head. I have never seen anything like it. He didn't even know where he was, what day of the week it was.

Sebastian who was the bar manager has jumped over the bar and helped him back up because he was everybody's favourite if you know what I mean, because he spent a lot of money in there. Everybody knew him and nobody could quite believe what had happened. Everyone was dumbfounded and Dom was like "well what did you want me to do?"

Anyway, luckily we loved them in the bar and they loved us and always had a good crack up, so nobody took sides and I kept wondering how we got to this stage, but anyway we left the bar.

The next day we drew up a bit of a battle plan cos Dom was thinking I hope there won't be trouble when we go back, can we go back? What's going to happen? and like. His other friend Wolfie who was a champion amateur boxer had come out at that point as well and he was there. We were all talking and said if we get any trouble you know you can help me, and he was like alright don't worry about that. We said Nick you can do what you can do.

As I said we went back to the bar expecting some sort of retaliation or something. Sebastian the bar man was fine and just said let's forget about what happened and I think Jean Paul walked in that night and walked through and we thought here we go, but he actually came over and apologised to Dom and said "I was out of order and didn't know what I was doing and that I had had a few drinks" and it was put to bed.

But like I said in all my years of being involved around those sorts of incidents, I have never seen anything like that or heard anything like that thud and had to actually turn my back. It made me feel physically sick, so powerful, so quick and I just thought wow, he is the real deal. It was unbelievable. I have never seen anything like it. I have never seen a bloke knocked out for that long. Jean Paul had that lump on his head for weeks and I bet he still gets headaches to this day.

Another story I could tell you was another night at Paddy's Bar, remember I was wet behind the ears back then, I was only 23/24. There were three Essex guys in there playing darts being a bit rowdy and that, but they knew Dom and it was like "hey Dom how you doing?" and they couldn't believe they'd seen each other. Anyway, I said what they doing over here Dom and he said they have come over here to do a job. I was thinking oh ok what kind of job lol, but obviously as I have got older and wiser and know a few more things, they were obviously over to do some debt collecting or something like that. It was a real mixing with the shady kinda night.

These guys didn't look like the kind of guys you wanted to mess with, but they had total respect for Dom. What a mad night to have all these guys in a bar in a little fishing port in Denia in Spain.

As I said I lost my missus, my job but had the best time of my life. We still keep in touch through social media and I can honestly say he is one of, if not the nicest blokes you will ever meet. You wouldn't want to get on his wrong side anyway and I am glad I am on his right side.

My missus can't believe I know him, when he came up on the tv when we were watching the hard men stuff, but I know the other side to him and I think he proper brilliant, he is ace.

He calls me the Northern Connection as I come from up North.

BUTCH GOLDHAWK
(Former Heavyweight Contender)

I met Dom in about 2006 or just a bit before. I knew about him before I had met him as I had watched the BBC1 documentary on him. I was an amateur boxer at the time I was 22. I wanted to go pro.

About three months later I went down to KO gym in Walthamstow with Noel Tierney and they bunged Dom in to train me. I had some of my unlicensed fights with Dom in my corner and our relationship went from there.

I was in awe of Dom. He is just a loveable giant really. He is always making people laugh. Don't get me wrong, if you upset him you know about it.

I definitely upset him once, it was 2012. I was a pro but was giving it up. Selling tickets for the fights done my head in, it was really hard. I told Dom I didn't want to do it anymore and he was like "yeah, whatever". About a month later Dillian Whyte had double booked his sparring. He was due to be sparring with Vitali Klitschko. They wanted me to go and spa with Rampage Jackson from the UFC. To be really honest I didn't want to go. All I wanted to do was stay at home and be with me kids. Dom was like "it is such a good opportunity". I really didn't want to do it, but they coaxed me into it. It was in Brazil.

On the Wednesday they called me to tell me they had booked my flight and I was going on the Friday. I remember speaking to Dom at the airport, I was all choked up having to go away for three weeks. I went from Heathrow to Portugal and then had to get a flight to Brazil. When I got there, I remember walking around the airport at 11pm with my two suitcases, and all I knew was I had to meet these two geezers who are from Liverpool.

I am walking around the airport thinking someone will be there holding a card up with my name on it, but nobody is there. I wait an hour. I am trying to use a payphone but don't know the dialling codes. Anyway, two hours now have gone past and I have got the hump. I go up to the desk and change my flight to come straight back home. The attendant was like "you have only just got here". I was like "I am here on my own, nobody has met me, I am going back home".

Anyway, I am lining up to get on the plane and a little Brazilian man runs up to me with a phone saying "your friends, your friends are outside, come on follow me". I was like "no I am getting on the plane". He passes me the phone and a Liverpudlian voice says "Come on, we got arrested on the way to the airport". I'm like "you think I am getting off the fucking plane, not a chance".

At the stop off again in Portugal I thought I would phone Dom. Oh my god, did he have the hump, that was it. First he has a go at me and then he goes into a sulk and then for three weeks after that he won't talk to me.

I go to the gym after that and he just will not talk. He won't even make eye contact with you. I know I really upset him. After a while he softens up and starts communicating with you. You know he doesn't want to fall out with you for forever, it's just that his emotions take over there and then and he can't control his them. He gets angry. After time and perseverance of me keep going to the gym and don't get me wrong it would have been easier not to have gone, but I did keep going. After a while he started to open up a little bit again and just calls me "a waste of space".

That story happened over 10 years ago but he still talks about it now.

About three years ago I went back to boxing as a journeyman, he fell out with me again then. To be fair to him, I went back to the boxing and wasn't in the right frame of mind and therefore wasn't training as well as I should have been. I was being an idiot. I was drinking when I shouldn't have been and wasn't taking my safety seriously. Dom did the right thing to be fair, he refused to be in my corner because I wasn't looking after me self. He didn't talk to me though and I had to go to the last couple of fights on my own.

Then randomly he turns up out the blue and it's all forgotten.

He has always been nice, it's just if you upset him he is not.

There are too many stories. Another time we went out for a Xmas do in Chingford. There was about 20 of us and we wanted to go to a bar across the road. The doormen was like "no, there are 20 of you and we are closing soon". Dom was like "whack" and we never were allowed in.

I remember sharing a room with him in Scotland. He snores!! He was snoring when he was still awake haha. I said "Dom you are snoring", he was like "so do you, you cunt". I was like "yes but I am asleep when I do it, you are still awake". I know he suffers with his sleep. When I go to sleep I like to turn the light off. He likes to sleep with the tv on though.

Another memory, I remember getting on a plane with him once. Picture two 20 stone men and they stuck us next to the smallest Chinese woman in the world. She must have been the unluckiest person on the plane. You know how everyone is looking at you when you walk down the aisle. It was funny.

I remember taking Dominic to work with me, I am a carpenter and pitch roofs. Dom was having a bad morning so we sent one of the young lads to the local convenient store and ended up getting pissed. As I said, so many different stories and situations we have shared.

I have met Bella a few times but don't see her as often now as she is working.

I am in awe of Dominic. I think he is a great man. I know he sometimes struggles emotionally, but that is just who he is.

He is always doing something for somebody else. I will be honest he always puts himself second. He is very loyal. I know if I needed something, I could call him up and he would come and do it.

THE SPARTA YEARS

"Loyalty is the main foundation"

IAN WILSON
(Sparta Gym Owner and Boxing Trainer)

I had heard and found out about Dom before I met him. I had a good friend that used to do some work with Dom.

However, I first met Dom years later through the boxing many years ago in the late 1990's and our friendship just went from there. I used to run and train a fella who fought Dom called Chris Henry, they had a Southern Area Title fight. Dom ended up winning the fight.

We opened a little gym together, going back in the day. He used to come in and train a couple of privates and our friendship just went from strength to strength really and we have been friends ever since.

We have a good stable friendship. We are not in each other's faces but we know we have each other's backs. We don't need words. Our friendship is around and revolves boxing.

As a boxer he was great. What beat Dom was Dom. He had a good relationship with his trainer but I think he went as far as he wanted to go and then just went the other way, the other side, which I choose not to talk about because that is his business.

Dom is as hard as nails. When you put someone in front of him to fight, nothing then phases him. But when he gets the normal run of the mill life problems, he struggles to deal with them. Some men are like that, they are hard men but the other end they are soft.

He got involved with something he should never have got involved with, if you know what I mean. He really wasn't that person. Sometimes one does things because your name is put up, but when your name is put up it can be taken down.

There are people that don't care, that don't hold their hands up. They just chop you into bits and throw you down the river. Sadly, when that lot is out the way there is another lot behind them and another lot, where does it all end? That's what Dom lives with in his head.

He has done things he shouldn't have done for the sake of other people and he lives by it now. It worries him. He doesn't stop worrying about it. Even now. You know if you don't want to regret something, don't do it. If you can't take the consequences, don't do the crime.

Dom has always been the same to me and always will be. He wears his heart on his sleeve. He can't get his head out of his ex which he should do and move on. He lives in the past a little bit and struggles to move on. That's the main trouble.

He should have a good woman behind him. He doesn't let that happen, sadly he just needs to let go of the past. I have told him many times he needs to get into a relationship and be with someone that truly cares for him and then he would have a different outlook.

The only thing that changes or can change Dom is Dom. In the way that, his daughter would know, she has seen the changes in him. He shows her more emotion than anybody I suppose.

I tell him all the time – move on. Let go of the past.

I love him dearly. He is my mate. Everyone loves him, but you can't help him. He is that man. What if?? what but???

BOB KIPPS
(Boxing Trainer)

I have known Dom for years and years, from when he was fighting, when he was the Milky Bar Kid. There is a big age gap between us. I was packing up whilst he was getting started.

He is just a friend now, we just talk.

Since having Bella he has become a lot calmer. He still has got it there when he wants to, but he has definitely calmed down a hell of a lot.

I really would just describe him as a good friend.

87

STEVE KIPPS
(Boxing Trainer)

I first saw Dom at the NE London Divisional Championships in the mid 1990's. Blonde curly hair, glasses and he didn't look a boxer and looked out of place. For some reason I always looked forward to him boxing as he was game and always committed 100%.

At that time, I knew nothing about him or his reputation it was purely his boxing and I followed his career when he turned pro and won the Southern Area title.

I then heard stories of his reputation.

A few years later I took a lad called Ian Napa sparring to the Five Star gym and as we walked in Dom was there with Lenny his coach. This was my first true encounter with Dom and despite my trepidation, was surprised at what a lovely welcoming he gave us and it was hard to put the reputation to the lovely, fun loving bloke we met.

We met a few more times at the Five Star gym and after that I didn't see him.

Fast forward 15+ years and I was without a gym and looking for some sparring for Matthew Chanda and was told of a lad that was being trained by Dom in Chingford at the Sparta Gym. I took a chance and popped along and found Dom sat with a group in the adjoining café.

I was worried he wouldn't remember me, but to my great surprise he boomed "It's Stevie Kipps, come here mate". He gave me the biggest bear hug and warm welcome as if I'd only seen him last week. And I think that sums Dom up … he doesn't forget you.

I've not looked back since that day and stayed based at Sparta ever since.

I've heard the stories about Dom but that's not the person I've known. He has always been respectful, but at the same time can be forceful in speaking his mind, so you know where you stand with him and I've never had a problem with that, or him.

There's mutual respect. And by that from my point of view I mean not only his boxing achievements and his knowledge of the sport, but most of all the fact that he wanted to turn his life around and has achieved that with hard work and commitment, just like he did in the ring.

He has a daughter, (Bella), you know, in case he's never mentioned it, lol, and is an excellent father wanting only the best for her. He wants her to respect the man he is, and not the man he was, and you can only admire him for that.

Dom has got a big heart and at times wears it on his sleeve.

He has helped raise money for good causes willingly giving his time and recently climbed back in the ring, and again that's truly admirable.

STUART POTAZNICK
(Welterweight Boxer)

When I first met Dom it was in the boxing gym and we were training side by side. Then he came to the end of his fighting career and he wanted to take on a few boxers, so he approached me and asked would I be interested in training with him. I said yeah of course so, we started training together.

There was one day I remember we were training together and I kept dropping my right hand. Dom said to me "if you keep dropping that right hand I'm gonna bloody give you a left hook". I was like "alright, alright". I kept going and there was this one time I dropped my hand and he has given me this left hook and smacked me straight on the nose.

At that time, I didn't even realise my nose was broke, but he had hit me with this left hook and I went "ooooh" looked back at him and I breathed through my nose, sniffed and said "Dom I think you have just sorted out my nose, it's all fine now". Dom just stood there staring at me and said "you little prick". We both stood staring at each other and then started laughing our heads off.

Another time I was training at the gym and Dom was training or doing pads or something. This geezer has come in and started training. Ian had offered to do some sparring with him. This geezer accepted his offer. He was nearly as big as Dom and Ian who in only about 5ft 6/7 and middleweight sort of class.

They got into the ring and the bloke started taking liberties with Ian. You could see Dom's face kept watching him training and you could tell he was thinking why is this guy taking such liberties with Ian. Ian being Ian can handle it and let him get on with it, but it starting to look like the big geezer was really loading up.

Dom's gone, "you know what, sod this", and has just gone over, grabbed his gloves and said "Ian, get out. I'll have a little spa with him". They started sparring and the bloke has gone to lump Dom and Dom just done a little one, two combinations with a left hook and basically sparked the geezer out, lol. "That sorted that out didn't it" he laughs.

We had a Christmas do, I can't remember what year it was but we got this Xmas night out and we were meant to be sharing a room. He had gone back to the room earlier as he obviously had had a few too many drinks and I stayed out. Later that evening when I went back to the room Dom was laying on the bed. I was all hyper as I'd been drinking. I was like jumping around and he was like "will you quieten down as you going to wake the neighbours". I was like "oh shut up it will be alright". I got down to me pants and that and was jumping around and I jumped off the edge of the bed and did a belly flop onto the floor. He has jumped up and got me, screaming "will you calm down". I thought he was going to choke me and I was like "yes Dom, I'll calm down" and jumped back straight into bed, haha.

He has always been a good friend to me. Whenever I think of him it's as my big cuddly friend.

WARREN BARNES
(Ex Boxer and Trainer)

I know Dom from boxing. The first time I ever met him was over 30 years ago. It was my first pro fight debut. He was in the same changing room as me.

I always found him a nice guy.

We kept meeting over the years on the pro circuit and now I train him. The more I train him the more we speak. It is a more intimate relationship now.

He is a tough guy, but he has a soft heart.

The picture people have got of him, (shakes his head), I get the real Dom. A gentle giant. He is a fiery character but is a good guy, a nice guy. I really like him.

He might not give people that impression, but he really is loving, caring and gentle.

I have seen him going from 100 to 0 in 10 seconds. I'm like "Come on Dom, Wow!". He is like smash up first and think later.

I have a lot of time for him and you know if you ever call him he will always be there. He will have your back. He is a loyal man.

He needs to start being loyal to himself.

KEITH DURSO
(Gym Companion)

I would say, I had heard of Dom, as I had been following boxing over the years, so I knew who he was.

The first time I ever met him and I will never ever forget it. Dom and his partner Ian Wilson were doing up the gym in Chingford and attached to the gym was a café. I was sitting in the café, I had never been in the gym before, I only used to go and do the golf in the driving range. I got talking to Ian, who was sitting in the café. We were both sitting at the table having a talk when all of a sudden, this giant came through the door, who was Dom.

He just stood next to the table looking down and because I was talking to Ian he just looked down and said "you alright mate?" and I looked up at this enormous fella and I just went "what do you wanna fight?" lol. He looked down and the three of us just burst out laughing and from that moment on me and Dom had a rapport and we got on.

I have so much respect for Dom over what he has done throughout the years, but from that moment on we just got on and it has been a pleasure knowing him. It really has. That was the first time I ever met him and I will never forget it, it is imbedded in me head. Me asking Dom if he wants a fight.

Through the way Dom is, he encouraged people to join that gym. I have never been in a gym like it, because if you go to one of the big gyms, you go in, don't talk to anyone and you just do a bit of training and go home. That gym wasn't like that. Because of the way Dom and Ian was you went in there and it was as much about the banter and Dom is a big one for giving out banter.

You won't get through the door without him taking the mickey out of ya, and it doesn't matter who you are, he will take the mickey out of everyone. But he will take it back as well.

Me and Dom got quite close over the years. Especially when his mum died. When she died he was sort of a bit lost I think. So, when he went out to Italy to bury his mum, because he knew as a taxi driver I used to work late, sometimes Dom would phone me 1am, 2am in the morning, just to talk, if he was lonely. To have someone there to talk to. He always knew and knows that if he ever needs someone to talk to he can phone me. I will always be there to talk to him.

I remember one night he phoned me up and I said "what you doing Dom?" and he said sitting in the room with me mum. I said "that's nice" and he said "yes, but I want to get next to her and give her a cuddle". The two of us just burst out laughing. I could just picture his poor mum lying there and he wants to get in bed and give her a cuddle. But that was him, very loving.

He has gone through some hard times but he has come out the other side as well. I think he has done well for himself.

You never know what you are going to get with Dom.

I remember one time we went for a Christmas do with the gym. I got a taxi down there and unbeknown to me as my taxi driver pulled into the car park he must have cut another driver up, coming the other way. The other driver pulled into the car park and as I got out the taxi to walk away the other driver has jumped out and he was a bit of a bully giving it to my taxi driver.

Dom came out and he started off trying to calm the man down saying "listen fella, it's Christmas time blah blah blah". The guy made a mistake, and had a verbal with Dom and it finished up with Dom chasing him around the car park.

He switched just like that, that is what I mean with him being unpredictable. One minute he is nice but he can switch just like that. But that's Dom, that's who he is and I accept that.

I think Dom is a lovely fella, he has had some hard times over the last few years. He has come out the other side and I think he is doing well for himself now. Hats off to him.

I will always consider Dom to be a good friend, always.

If Dom doesn't like what I have said about him "fuck him" haha!!

JIM HEMMINGS
(Friend)

I will start from the beginning. I first met Dom through a situation 11 years ago. My dad had passed away very suddenly, and I was a little bit lost in all honesty, I was all over the place. My dad was a huge, massive boxing fan so I thought I would have a charity boxing match to try and say goodbye to him because I didn't get a chance to because it was so quick.

I started looking for a gym, I was looking around couldn't find anything local to me. Sparta Gym came up which Dom Negus was there and Ian Wilson.

I remember I walked into the gym, met Dom. I knew the name obviously but didn't know anything about Dom apart from he was this big fearsome guy, that was connected to the underworld and so on. I was a bit apprehensive when I met him but I was at the stage where I was completely lost.

However, what greeted me was this great big teddy bear of a man, cracking the worse jokes you could have ever heard in your life, but you went along and laughed at them, because you are being polite.

In that time of training me for the charity fight, the guy became like a brother of mine. Even to this day, I still don't think he knows the impact he had on my life. He picked me up without knowing, kept me going. He gave me a reason to wake up in the morning with a smile, even though I was going through what was ridiculous trauma for me. I had that thing that gave me the spark in the day, because I knew I was going to see him. You know what I mean.

As I said when he talks he is very passionate, very animated, gets so animated because he has such a big heart.

When he talks about his daughter, you see his eyes light up. He is a very passionate guy. Not being funny you look at him and think he looks like a big scary fella, but I suppose when needed he could still be a handful, but for me that's the last thing.

He took someone that was completely lost and gave me focus and helped me get through the worst period of my life. Without sounding dramatic - it really was. He was there for me without knowing. I entered the gym as a complete stranger and when I left this guy was a brother to me and he will be for the rest of my life.

We keep in touch with messages and spoke for the first time recently after a couple of months. We have that type of thing, if I haven't spoken to him for a little while when we do, we are back on the phone. Still with terrible jokes, the worst jokes I have ever heard.

He is a really big guy with a really big heart.

I actually said it to him the other day "I don't think you understand what you done for me" and he was like "AH OH YEAH" in his cockney way of talking. I said "you really don't understand, for you to do that to someone who was a total stranger, what you did and how you picked me up and kept me going".

Literally he is my brother. I will never tire talking about Dom he is one of life's good people.

All the goodness that comes his way is well deserved.

DAVE GIBO GIBSON
(Friend)

I met Dom in 2012, I was living in Dubai, originally from Leeds and then I moved to Essex. I am a rugby player you see. A few months before I had dislocated my knee playing rugby and the doctor said I wouldn't be able to play again for nine months to a year, as I wasn't allowed any contact on my knee. My mate Max took me to the gym because I thought I would try boxing instead.

Max knew Dom and he took me down to Dom's gym where we did a training session with him. I remember the first time I met him, we shook hands. I am 6ft2 and 100kg and his hands were like two of my hands. They just swamped my hand. He is like a giant human. I think he has got freakish strength, that's why he punches so hard. He is just a genetic freak of nature.

After our first training session, Dom had a chat with me and said if I wanted to go to the gym and train, he would help me get some fights and stuff. And that's literally how we met.

After that I saw him basically every day for the next year. I was in the gym nearly every single day, training with Dom, apart from Sundays.

As a trainer he constantly took the piss out of me, all the time. If you speak to anyone about Dom, they will all say he is a big piss taker. He is the life and soul. He was the life and soul of that gym, that is Dom all over.

Dom took me from a person that had never boxed before in my life to fighting on the unlicensed cards. He turned me into, I wouldn't call myself a decent boxer, but I could throw a punch.

We had a good group at the gym, it was like a family. I didn't really know anyone in the area in Essex and I went down there and made loads of friends, a huge social group

95

straight away.   It saved me from leaving Essex. It was a great gym, busy all the time. There were lots of taxi drivers there during the day. I have been to quite a few gyms since and I have never experienced the atmosphere as I got there. Ian who ran the gym was lovely, but Dom was the life and soul of the gym. He is just one of those people that everyone likes. He is always funny. Even if you are having a bad day, Dom would take the piss out of you and you would leave happy.

Obviously, I have heard stories about Dom's reputation and stuff, but I never saw it. In the gym and when he was training me he was always super nice. Our friendship went on from there. I always got on with Dom. He is quite an emotional person and so am I.

There aren't many stories to tell but I remember when he was training for his fight, he just used to sit on the rowing machine and row for an easy half an hour non-stop. I don't know if people are aware but if ever you use a rowing machine it burns everywhere when you get on it after two minutes. So, to sit on it for 30 minutes and just row at a good pace is just freakishly strong.

The first time I went out drinking with Dom, I think it was the Christmas do. I had only known him for a few weeks then. We had been there about half an hour and someone, I can't remember the guy's name, got up and gave a speech. He said something that Dom didn't like and Dom basically just flipped a table over, lol, ran over and open handed slapped this guy. I was like oooh and ouch what had just happened?.

I boxed for Dom for a couple of years, then left and moved back to Dubai. I always kept in touch with Dom. I called him one day and he was a bit down. He had split with Nic (Bella's mum) so I said out the blue why don't you come to Dubai. Literally an hour later he rang me to say he had booked a ticket and was coming to spend a week with me. It was really nice to have him there.

If it wasn't for Dom's daughter Bella, Dom might not be here. It is awful to think of, but Dom can be in that sort of mindset. He has a lot of PTSD from his past and a lot of demons.   Bella saved him.   She saved him till this day probably.

LYLE GORNALL – GINGER
(Friend and Ginger Viking)

I met Dom back in 2016 at Serious Fitness in Nazeing. I was training with another trainer and Dom used to come in with his boys for training sessions. I used to stay after my own sessions to watch Dom do pads with them and would show them the ropes about boxing to add to their arsenal. Tell them how they can get better and certain shots etc. I literally used to just hover around.

My trainer at the time, Jonny Camp, was one of Dom's best mates and that's how I got my introduction to Dom. I remember doing pads with him once, he absolutely petrified the life out of me. Because of who he was and what he was I so wanted to impress him. He kept saying to me "Lad stop being so tense, just relax. I wouldn't put you on the pads for no reason". I felt so honoured.

Jonny went off and wasn't training anymore and I really wanted to continue fighting. I called Dom up and said "I know you only really train pro's but is there any chance I can tag along and join in?". He said "Yes, but only on the condition you don't ever give up. I will tell you when you have had enough". On the odd occasion, he did.   He took a shot on me though and I am grateful for that.

He is like an older brother and a father figure all in one to me. It is just the way he is. I tell him personal home life stories and he always suggests ways to help. He is like a shoulder to lean on.

You get the laughy, jokey side of Dom first thing in the morning, before training at 5am. You know this absolute giant, screaming and shouting at you from across the gym making everyone laugh whilst you are getting ready and then, bang, seriousness the moment he starts training you.

He would always do something funny or silly. He has a great humour. I told him the most stupid joke about an owl once and he thought it was absolutely hilarious. He was in stitches for ages. "One of my good pals is really passionate about owls". Dom asked "Who?" and then he got the joke. Honestly the shittiest dad joke, he found it hysterical.

He used to just be the joker of the gym. Making silly noises and faces. A guy called Pat once walked in and Dom was like "Oh Pat" and the guy turns round and Dom says to him "Oh fuck off" haha. It is just Dom's character, just the way he is. When you are in the gym at 5am you need a personality like that.

This is a quite heartfelt moment, but I remember when we were training in Spain in Mercier I kept saying to Dom throughout the day my partner Jem has got to get a pregnancy test, we think it's happened. I remember sitting in the apartment with Dom and my phone rung and it was her and Dom looked at me and said "Go on mate, answer it, you know what's about to happen now…."

He literally gave me that nod, I burst into tears before even answering the phone and yes, she was pregnant. Dom was the first person that knew. A special moment we shared.

Another funny memory I have is we were training at the track with some of the other boys and Floyd Mayweather turned up. Dom told his entourage to fuck off. They thought we were spies for Liam Walsh who was fighting Gervonta Davis. They kind of turned up and we all stopped running. We saw this guy in a TMT hat and realised it was Floyd. Dom was like "Why the fuck have you all stopped running??". We were like "Dom, that is Mayweather", to which he replied "I don't give a fuck who it is, you are training mate, you focus on you".

His entourage tried to get us all off the track, Dom just told them to fuck off. Once Mayweather's lot realised half the boys there were on his undercard, they relaxed and started chatting away. It was a real surreal moment.

We always used to go to the café after training, but only for a "good breakfast". No fry up, always a Mediterranean breakfast, Dom's favourite.

I only have good precious memories of Dom.

I have spent time with Dom and Bella. I remember my first unlicensed fight I had under Dom it was at the Circus Tavern. Bella was about 11, she drew lots of pictures for me which Dom gave me before the fight.

Dom is an amazing father. He would do anything for his daughter, he would go to the end of the world for her. There is nothing out of reach when it comes to Bella.

Dom has definitely got calmer over the years. He hasn't changed personality wise, he is still the same Dom, just calmer in certain situations. He is as true as the sky is blue. He can still throw his toys out of the pram, he loves to. Everyone knows Dom is a big baby who needs a cuddle and reassurance at times. He is no different from anyone else out there. We all need an arm around us sometimes and just because he is 6ft 6 and built like a bear does not mean he is not insecure or vulnerable like all of us.

DAVE DENT AND DAVID YEARDLEY
(Gym Friends)

About nine years ago I first walked into the gym, I said "I want to do white collar boxing", I had never boxed in my whole life. Dom was sitting behind the counter. Dom basically got up, jumped on me as such, introduced himself, this was December 2, he said "right you are on, you are in, there is a White Collar event on April 2". This was a long time ago.

He is just always there. When Dom is in the gym there is just a different atmosphere. He is larger than life. You always hear him. You know when he is coming through the door.

"Are we allowed to swear?", they ask me. There is always some cunt in the corner if Dom is in there. "Dave, fuck off".

He stinks the bog out sometimes. If he goes in there, it's the whole of that end of the gym done. World War 1 and mustard gas has got nothing on Dom.

My son is 15, he absolutely loves Dom. Dom always has time for him. He always has a laugh and joke with him.

He always tries to bring the youngsters through. He always gives someone his time, jumps and hugs you, or runs you over lol.

I hope he doesn't hit me if I describe him as big, fat and ugly lol.

Larger than life would be another description of him.

He really is a lovely bloke. He is always here for you. Always has a listening ear. You can really chat with him quite deeply sometimes as well.

OREN YEARDLEY
(Gym Friend)

I met Dom about a year ago at Sparta gym. I go there with my dad, I am 15. I knew nothing about him until I met him.

He does swear a lot lol, he walks into the gym and if it's ok to swear, he says to me "hello you c***", but he does it with a smile on his face. He always has time for me.

He has this long running joke with me. He says "do you want to come and see the puppies in the back of my car or I have got some sweeties" haha. It makes me laugh.

I would say Dom is joyful, scary and quite big.

THE FIGHTING YEARS

"It is better to stand and fight, if you run you will only die tired"

STEVE BUNCE
(Television and Radio Sport Pundit and Newspaper Columnist)

Dark alleys, pubs, doors, streets and gyms are where most Dominic Negus tales start and end. I have a different one.

In about 2011, Dom was a studio guest on my BBC Radio London Show. I think he had just been profiled somewhere in one of those Hardmen TV Shows. Others now knew a little bit about the man.

He did his 30 minutes and was funny, serious, sharp and polite. It was a smarter Dom than the knock-your-door-down Dom. Nobody in the studio could believe it was the same man they had read about or heard about. I knew about that loyal man, that friend.

Dom talked about the Audley fight, other hard fights, not making the most of his boxing skills, being attacked. Being hated and feared and trying to be a good person. It was great stuff. He could have hosted a show, he was that good.

Anyway, I never told the people I worked with that Dom left the studio that night and had to drive to the Essex coast to knock on a door and make a collection. "It was fucking messy, I had to be a bit lively" he told me later.

One night, one man and two very, very different sides. I guess that is what makes dangerous men different.

IAN JOHN LEWIS
(British Boxing Referee)

Dominic Negus was on the boxing circuit after I retired quite a few years ago and became a referee. I remember Dominic as being the Milky Bar Kid and in his early days he would chuck out milky bars at everyone. It was quite comical, quite amusing and quite a good thing. Then he progressed to, and I am not sure if he was, Southern Area Champion, but him and Garry Delaney fought for the Southern Area Title. This was 6th October 2000 at Maidstone Leisure Centre.

I had not long been a top referee. But because of their nature, Garry Delaney was one tough guy and Dominic Negus was also a tough guy. Before I got in the ring, world class referee, Roy Francis, what a lovely guy he was and was one of my mentors said to me "Ian, be on top of this as this could get right out of hand". I said "Roy, if I can't handle this fight, then I can't handle World Title fights". Sure enough it was a war. They punched lumps out of each other, they talked, taunted and gave it large to each other during the fight. But they respected themselves and me which helped me keep on top of it and it was a good fight. That is my first recollection of refereeing Dominic Negus.

I then refereed Dominic again 26th May 2001 when he KO'd Paul Aske in the 1st round.

What a lot of people will remember me and Dominic Negus for was me being the referee and Dominic fighting the 2000 Olympic medallist Audley Harrison. He had signed a £1,000,000 deal with the BBC. He demanded to be top of the bill. His first 10 fights were being shown live on BBC which was absolutely fantastic back in the day. They thought Audley Harrison was the next Lennox Lewis. Unfortunately he wasn't, but was still a very good fighter!!!.

Sure enough came fight number six of ten and I got the call to be told I would be refereeing Audley Harrison against Dominic Negus 10th July 2002. I thought fantastic!!! Absolutely brilliant.

I remember going to the dressing room to give them their pre-fight instructions. Seeing Dom and going "look at the size of you". He was a monster. He was a cruiserweight and had to put weight on. Audley Harrison is a big lump, 6ft 5 and a good 18 stone. Dom was like "I had to put a few pounds on mate to take this guy on".

We had a nice chat. It was at Wembley Arena and the place was absolutely packed. There were lots Audley fans and lots of Dominic Negus fans too.

Dominic Negus fancied his chances because no one had beaten Audley Harrison, people had come close.

I'm not exactly small, but I was like a right little boy compared to these two lumps in the ring.

The fight started and Audley dominated the fight. Dominic keeps coming forward, he had to cos he is the smaller guy. He has tried to rough him up, give it to him. But Audley is boxing smartly, on the back foot, keeping Dominic under control ish. Dominic gave it a good go. In the 4th round, half way through, Harrison caught Dominic with a nice left hand, bang. He hit, he hurt him, he backed off and then because he hurt him, Negus dipped.

He didn't actually put his knee on the floor, but he dipped by the ropes and thinks I will take a breather.

In the rules of boxing if no part of your body is touching the canvas the referee doesn't count, the time keeper doesn't count. He has knelt down by the ropes, nothing is touching the floor. Neither me nor the time keeper has counted. Audley Harrison has looked at him and thought, what is he doing? I will smash him again then. And he hit him again.

With that Dominic Negus has felt disrespected, "I am down, you have hit me, now you are going to get it". With that he has leapt up, he has come flying forward, took the gumshield out of his mouth and he tried to nut Audley Harrison badly.

Thankfully because Audley is quite tall, he leaned back and he didn't connect. If he had connected I would have had no choice but to disqualify Dominic Negus, then it would have all kicked off, no doubt. There would have been a massive fight and everything. That is my personal opinion and the opinion of a lot of other people. As I said, it didn't connect, but obviously the intention was there big time.

Audley has grabbed him, Dominic has tried to break through. I am trying to get in between them because Dominic has done a foul. I am trying to get between them, these lumps, they are trying to fight each other. Anyway, I have got to get between them and finally managed to split them up and get Audley to the neutral corner.

Dominic's going from corner to corner, snarling madly and I am following him shouting at him saying "do you know what you have done here, do you know what you have done?" He was like "yeah yeah, of course", staring right at Audley. Obviously the crowd are absolutely loving it, the Dominic Negus crowd. They are egging him on. He's loving it. I am thinking I need to get this big guy under control because he is losing it.

I work for the Kent police, in the cells, so I am used to dealing with irate prisoners and calming them down, also being an ex-fighter me self helped.

Dominic was absolutely livid and he wanted some of Audley Harrison. I knew I had to get this guy under control. I thought I am not going to disqualify him as there would be absolute mayhem, so, I kept shouting at him "look at me, look at me Dominic". He sort of looked at me and I thought I have his attention now. I dropped his gumshield on the floor and I said "Is that your gumshield?" and it distracted him and he went "Yeah". I was like "good, lets get it, get it cleaned and do what you do best ..... fight". He was like "Yeah alright".

So, I took him to his trainer, where he put the gumshield back into his mouth. I sent Dominic to a neutral corner.

I went to Audley who had been waiting patiently in the neutral corner, I gave him a bollocking "when I try to break you apart, you break apart, you understand?" and he was like "yeah yeah sorry". It was like right let's get them together and get back on with the fight. The fight continued. The bell went they went back to their corners. The next two rounds were under control and quite evenly fought. Thank God it ended, they smiled at each other and went their own ways.

What was funny was when they got interviewed Dominic said "I couldn't get to him, he is too damn big, with his long arms but anyway he can't hit very hard, my mum hits harder than that". Haha

After that fight Dominic tested positive for steroids, to get him that size for that fight. If I remember rightly he refused to pay the fine and ended up banned professionally and only allowed to fight on the white collar circuit.

I remember when I got out of the ring, the time keeper, Nick White, an ex-referee said to me "Ian, Ian. I don't know what you said to them but thank God you got it under control. I was ready to dive under the ring, because I knew it was going to kick right off. You did fantastic". I really appreciated that.

Some referees said to me they would have instantly disqualified Dominic, but if I had done that it would have been carnage and the BBC cameras would've loved it as bad news is good news. If Dominic had gone boom and got right in there and had actually cut him, I would have had no choice. But I had to take that chance.

My common sense and my fight sense, I sensed I did the right thing. The crowd were incensed. After Nick said that to me, I knew I had done the right thing.

I made history in 2000. I am the first British black international boxing referee ever. I am very proud of that.

It is amazing Dom is doing this book. He is awesome. Dominic has been in my book and it is very nice to be in his.

STEVE LILLIS
(Boxing Journalist and Commentator)

I had heard all the stuff about Dom and have read his books, and know what he has been like, but I can honestly say in all my dealings with him he has been superb.

When he was boxing professionally, I went to a lot of his fights, interviewed him and was fantastic to deal with. You know what, I miss not seeing him ringside now not doing the security. There would always be a joke or piss take or something, a one liner.

The other side of Dominic, I don't know whether you call it insecurity or sensitivity even when he has been a lunatic, there has been a real sensitive side to him. People have this lunatic impression of him, but there is quite a soft guy in there. He beats himself up over a lot.

I remember one time, I can't remember the exact fight he was working at doing security, but it was in Liverpool, it might have been the Derek Matthews v Stephen Ormond title 2013. He was at the press conference that week and was going through a real, real hard time.

I think his relationship had broken up and it was his concerns about his daughter. I had about an hour with him really pouring it out to me, about how he was feeling and he was so low, really real low. He feared that he may not have the access to his daughter that he wanted, and it was a real other side to him.

About two days later he came up to me and said "Steve, that done me real good talking to you the other day" and it was a really deep conversation that he was coming out with and he was doing most of the talking. You know it was like someone in one of those AA meetings that wanted to share something and he shared it with me. It was in the hotel opposite Liverpool Arena it might have been at Durys Inn and it was about three days before the fight. He must have been doing the security all week up there and it was a real other side to him.

The grudge I have seen him carry, even though we now haven't discussed it for a few years was obviously the final fight against Audley Harrison; it didn't end well. You know the result and he nutted Harrison and lost the fight and then tested positive for steroids – I don't think he turned up for the second hearing after the initial test - got banned for life - it was a shit time for him.

I have never heard him speak worse of any other boxer than Audley. There was something afterwards when Audley wouldn't let Dom's dad go and meet him in the dressing room, and I think that's the one person he still mentions years on. Even though it was a long time ago, it's probably now a decade since he's mentioned it to me, but he was still carrying what happened that night. I got the impression he really carried dislike for Audley from that incident.

I have only briefly discussed this next thing with Dom, but you know what, he was so hurt when he split with Boy Jones Junior. The wound of that did a lot to him. I think he was hurt cos I know he did a lot for Boy JJ. When he was training him, it was like 'me and my shadow'. Boy JJ wasn't quite mini me as he didn't have Dom's growling personality but wherever Dom was, he took that kid with him, to Spain and all over the place. I don't know the ins and outs and I know there are two sides to every story and I am not taking sides to what went wrong, but I know he was really hurt.

I know he has a tough guy image, but there has been a lot in his life that hasn't been violence that has left him wounded and hurt him inside. I remember him talking to me and sharing the grief he was going through of his relationship breaking up and his daughter, she was eight or nine then maybe younger. That tore him up.

You know what, I have heard people moan about him but I can't say a bad word about him. He has always been good to me and there really is a lot more to him than this hard ex-gangland enforcer or whatever persona. There is another side to him and you wonder if there are still things inside him now that are tearing him up, it makes me wonder. I haven't seen him for a while but when I think of him I wonder if he is troubled, or whether he is at peace sometimes.

No one knows what truly goes on in someone else's mind and if he is still torn apart not spending as much time with his daughter as he did. He still might be bitter towards Audley Harrison - he might not let that resentment go.

He has mentioned it a couple of times since the conversation we had about his daughter, but I haven't seen him so much lately because our paths go in different ways, but we have the odd telephone call and they are the sort of things I think of with him.

As for his boxing career, I wonder did he get as far as he should of got. Maybe so in the sense that he got a Southern Area title, won a double WBU Intercontinental title, beat a couple of good fighters, lost to Bruce Scott who was a very good fighter but I wonder about the Chris Henry fight, whether he was ever the same after that as I think he only ever won one of his next four fights after that. His career wasn't as good, as I think he was unbeaten going into the Chris Henry fight, but after that he fought better fighters but wasn't winning as often as he could have before that fight. Again, that might be something else, he has never discussed that with me, but ask him.

That sensitive side is definitely there, whether that sensitivity is caused through you know insecurity or hurt he feels. I don't know, I'm not a psychologist. I'm sure a psychologist would love to have an hour with him, lol, they would need about a month with him. That's my take on him as a person away from boxing anyway.

Dom may disagree with me, but I am just speaking as I find because I always got on with him. I have heard people moaning about him, but in boxing everyone moans about everyone. (laughs) There is no sport more bitchy, they can be smashing you to bits one day and then got their arm around your neck giving you a big hug. Most people in boxing you wouldn't want behind you with a porcupine I tell you!

KUGAN CASSIUS
(Founder of iFilm)

In my twenties I had heard Dominic's name. I had watched things and read his name in books. I was fascinated with that whole scene. I always knew who he was. We did have mutual friends back then even though I was younger.

He might not remember our first meeting but I do, it was at an unlicensed fight of his in Manchester with a guy called Chris Bacon about 2008/2009.

In about 2010 I got involved with the media side of boxing and that's when me and Dom became friends.

As I said, I had known about him way before I met him. I am from Essex and Dominic has had a lot of connection to Essex in somewhat form.

I don't remember the first time I met him what I thought, but from the meeting in 2010 it took me a good couple of years to I can't say work Dom out, because I don't think there is anyone on the planet that has quite worked Dom out yet, but I think what I did quickly realise is Dom is one of them people that perception is one thing.

People have read stories, heard stories, seen things on tv etc, have been given a misleading view of him in my eyes.

For the first couple of years I used to go to his Chingford gym and interview and film his guys that he used to train. That is how my thoughts of him began to develop.

With Dominic if he is your friend you only see that side of him and don't want to take him for anything more than that.

I know this tough guy perception of him is warranted. However, my relationship with Dom has always been on a friend side. We have always only got on over that many amount of years. That is really the only side I have ever taken any notice of of him, if that makes sense.

With Dom, where we have been around the boxing scene for that first period, for me he has been one of those people that I will know and do know that from day one until the rest of our years as someone that if I needed help, and when I say help, I do not mean in the physical way would always be there.

I mean Dom has always put himself out for me emotionally. This is something I do not get from a lot of people in boxing, and I think where Dom has been through the mill in every category in life, he has been there on various occasions for me when I have had goings on in my personal life. He has always put himself out there.

Dominic has a sixth sense. He could read a post of mine that means nothing to anyone. Dominic can quickly realise something is not right, it might not be anything majorly wrong, 99% of people wouldn't see it. He is probably the 1% that can identify with it.

I have never rung Dom saying "this is going on and that's going on". We could literally have had a conversation and a week later he would phone up and say "we had that chat when we saw each other how's this now or that?" So, to me when I think of Dom and what he is to me, that is what my thing is with him. I can talk to him on that level which in boxing is kind of strange as it's all about egos and alpha males.

Recently I was going through a bad time, I had posted something, again, Dom picked up on it. It's like he senses it. "I need to check on him, it's not like him, that doesn't sound right". I really didn't want to speak or respond to anyone. He messaged me but I was in a phase where I was ignoring everyone. He did not stop messaging me, until I responded to him and this was literally over three days. He was like "all you need to do is tell me you are alright, just send an emoji or something". I ignored and you could tell he was getting agitated/worried. It was like "Kug, I have messaged you 15 times now, just let me know you alright".

Eventually I replied and said I will speak to you when I can. He was "it's alright, it's all I wanted to know". That sticks with me with Dom. It's like he was on me and he didn't even know what it was. I don't even have that sort of relationship with many people in my life let alone in an industry that was so male driven. It very unique.

We also have a good wind up and banter, but for me that part of him is unique. I don't think a lot of people see that side of him and would be surprised to know that's what I think of him, as that type of person to me in my life.

Don't get me wrong he is fearless. If I was in a situation with 50 men with swords outside my door, if I could pick one person, I would pick up the phone and say "Dom there is 50 people outside and it's just me and you". You know he would already be on his way.

I have seen his sensitive side in different situations over the years and his emotional side too. He is a bit like the old Ronseal advert "Does Exactly what it says on the Tin". Dom is what he is. Heart on his sleeve. Says exactly what he thinks. He wouldn't say to me something to cater to my ego or because he thinks it's what I want to hear. He is like that across the board with everyone.

I have not been around with him and his girl, Bella, but I have heard so much about her from him.

The point I wanted to make was even reading, seeing things and hearing stories about Dom I have only and will ever only judge him as I find him to me. I have not got one negative thought or view on Dom.

KELLIE MALONEY
(Ex Manager and Promoter)

I was the promoter/manager for Dominic Negus for a number of years. I always found him easy to deal with.

He never questioned his opponents and if anything he was what I would call a real old classic boxer. He would turn up, have a fight, take his money and just smile. He was a true warrior. Very easy to work with.

I believe in his training he accepted the words of his trainer. He never questioned anything.

I remember him saying "my job is to fight, your job is to get me the fights and pay me the most money". Hopefully that is what I have done for him.

He fought Chris Henry for the Southern Area Title, which he won. It was one of the best fights I recall of his. They were both fighters that I promoted. They were nominated to fight each other, but it was a real good fight a war. I think that fight took so much out of Dominic and I think that is maybe one of the reasons he never progressed much more after that.

He was a good guy to work with and all I can say is he has the heart of a lion and the mind of a warrior.

Dominic is fearless, courageous, mad and funny. I believe anyone who wants to fight is mad. You can be sure that Dominic would have to be carried out before losing a fight, I have never known him to quit.

His personality was really funny, a great funny character.

He was as fearless as being a security guard at boxing shows as he was as a fighter. He was always there. If ever

I was in an argument, the person behind my back, standing by my shoulder was Dominic Negus. That is so true. He would be behind me saying "You alright?, you alright?".

He is just a real character.

ED ROBINSON
(Presenter and Producer Sky Sports)

When I used to box it was Eddie Robinson.

I kind of quite empathise with Dominic's story on a much lower, lesser level. He talks about being the kid who was picked on and having a few demons and suddenly finding boxing. Fighting gave him an outlet.

My story is similar, because I was quite asthmatic as a kid and couldn't do any sport. I was kind of full of testosterone and anger and probably self-hatred as well, and then found my way into boxing into a boxing gym. I boxed amateur and a couple of pro fights but I wasn't really any good. I just did it, you know I am quite proud of what I achieved and where I came from but it was low level kind of stuff.

I first met Dominic Negus when I worked then for Frank Maloney, I refer to Frank as Frank even though he is Kellie now, and I don't mean any disrespect by that, but the person I knew was Frank back then. Frank was a boxing promoter who had Lennox Lewis, although he was kind of his licensed manager Lennox was looked after by many different people. Frank was a kind of hustler really, who was looking to kind of create another champion to take over from Lennox. He was using the fact that Lennox was such a big name to draw other fighters in.

This first part might sound more about me, but I am just setting the scene.

What happened was a friend of mine phoned up Frank to ask if he could interview Lennox Lewis for his school magazine. Frank being in a good mood said if you are a fan of boxing why don't you come and help out in the office. The guy said my mate is an amateur boxer and mad keen on boxing and can recite the Boxing Yearbook, that was me. That's how I got involved in boxing.

113

It was great. The office was a very exciting environment. I started work there when I was at university. I worked for the Lennox Lewis/Frank Bruno fight in 1993 and after finishing my degree Frank said "come work in the office until you find a proper job".

I was pretty much hooked working in the office. I had my ear close to the ground with the amateurs because I was still boxing at the time and knew who everyone was. I was able to help steer Frank to get some of the best amateur prospects to turn professional.

If you have a great amateur pedigree, you have a much better chance of becoming a professional boxer and being successful at it. Even though amateur and professional boxing are very different, it's like doing T20 cricket and doing a test match, they are different. But if you have that pedigree and you show how good you are, you have got a pretty good chance of replicating it.

We signed up loads of good fighters. There was Peter Richardson, he won a Commonwealth Games Gold Medal. Paul Ingle who called himself the Yorkshire Hunter, Alan Temple, David Starie.

Then Dominic Negus came to the office. He had no amateur pedigree to talk of at all. I think Frank knew Lenny his trainer, who was very well respected. Generally, you wouldn't take a punt on someone who didn't have that amateur pedigree. Dominic, as soon as he come into the office had charm, charisma and something about him. I think Frank liked him because he was pretty much down to earth, the opposite of media trained, let's say.

Lenny, his trainer, was obviously like a father figure to him and didn't say too much, but Dominic had all this bravado character and just charmed us all.

Between us all we came up with the idea of him being 'The Milky Bar Kid'. When he was boxing he would throw out Milky Bars to the crowd. It was just a gimmick really but it meant he was an attraction to the bill.

Basically, for a promoter they have to decide if the fighter is someone they invest in or it's someone who has to take care of themselves financially. By that if a manager thinks

114

a fighter is going to end up a champion, they will often need to subsidise them the whole way through.

Because Dominic hadn't done too much as an amateur he had to sell a lot of tickets to really cover his and his opponent's purse. There was a lot of pressure on him straight away, and it almost felt like he was learning on the job. He had a few wins and was very popular. We all liked him and he was great fun.

I remember his fight with Chris Henry and Chris ending up in quite a bad way afterwards. After that Dom's head was not entirely in his fights. Frank Maloney realised Dom wasn't going to be the superstar or a massive attraction. I think that is when the dream died a bit for Dominic, and then eventually he went a different way with everything.

I carried on seeing Dominic all the time, because he would do the security and we would do the security with him. He started piling on the pounds and got bigger and bigger and ended up this tough guy, Santa Clause figure, with a bit of a beard a gruff smile, but still with a heart of pure kindness.

I cannot think of one moment when I have seen Dominic that I haven't completely enjoyed his company because he is just a proper, proper person. I have worked in boxing all my adult life. I have been at Sky for 23 years just doing boxing, working as a reporter, presenter and now as Senior Producer behind the scenes. I have met a lot of tough guys with interesting personalities. Dominic is probably one of the most interesting of the lot.

To the tail end of his career doing the unlicensed stuff, I mean he was a very successful unlicensed boxer, but I think he was almost playing the game there a little bit. He knew enough from his boxing career to look after himself, but I just remember him back in 1996 fighting as a fresh-faced kid, with dreams and seeing where it would take him.

Dominic is one of those people who I would describe as an onion. He is very much multi layered. On the outside you have this laughing exterior, charismatic character, but obviously he has some demons, issues and aggression.

When you go right down to the very centre of the onion, what is in his very core is something quite beautiful.

Dominic is someone who even though I don't speak to him all the time, if I see him at a show, I give him a hug and cuddle and we catch up on our families.

He is one of these rare people that I have met in boxing who I know if I phoned him at 2am and he was 50 miles away and I needed him, and I am not talking about for defending me, I mean if something terrible had happened to me or one of my family, I know he would be there for me, because he is just such a loyal, caring person.

I have known that about Dominic almost from day dot. He is one of these people that if you are his enemy you are his worst enemy, but if you are his friend he would always put you first. He has this absolute kindness about him, and that's at the very very centre of the onion. But as I say there is a lot of layers between that.

He is complicated and if he had been more middle class he would have ended up seeing a therapist and would have found out more about himself. Maybe given him certain coping mechanisms or more perception when he has gone down the wrong kind of way of life. He would play that down if he heard this now, he would make a joke as a deflective.

Without getting too deep now I think if you are not careful you can fall down a rabbit hole with your own behaviour. Where you do something, you feel bad for it, even though you put it in a little box and wrap it up or try not to look at it, but it's there and it makes you dislike yourself, so you do something else to make you dislike yourself more. I think a lot of times in life those kinds of people end up having to draw a line in the sand and have to forgive themselves for it and start being nice to themselves.

There are quite a few Born Again Christians in boxing. It's like they have done some bad things and almost just draw a line and say "I forgive myself for all that, God forgives me for all that. What matters is how I treat people from now on".

I think Dominic has gone through a few episodes of that in his life, where I think he has tried to forgive himself but has got drawn into stuff again.

I do feel like when you see someone with their child you find out what they are really like and about. I have spent quite a lot of time with a boxer in Belfast called Eamonn Magee and he was a proper proper tough guy. When I saw him playing in the garden with his kids you see into someone's soul a little bit. I have to say whenever I talk to Dominic and seeing him light up when he talks about his daughter and how much he loves her, you can just see he is intrinsically a good person.

My relationship with Dominic and this is true of everyone who has treated him well or with respect, is that he is a friend. One of those few that you can count on one hand of having in life. To be honest, they are more common in boxing than they are in normal life. Like I say you treat people as you find them and I just think the world of him. I think he is an amazing individual and human being and the only person he has ever tried to hurt is himself.

There's a saying in an old poem called The Minstrel by James Beattie that always makes me think of Big Dom.

"Zealous, yet modest; innocent though free; Patient of toil, serene amidst alarms; Inflexible in faith, invincible in arms."

BOB LONKHURST
(Author and Close Friend)

Although Dom and I have moved in very different circles we seemed to click almost from the day we met. By that time in about 1995, I was well established as a Boxing Board Inspector and regular promotions I worked were at York Hall, Bethnal Green.

Dom was a regular member of the security team working the front entrance. He knew who I was and his usual greeting was "Alright mate, keeping it in your trousers?". I soon realised that was part of his East End sense of humour and within a short time we often stood and chatted, provided it didn't interfere with his job.

Boxing was obviously the main topic of conversation especially as he was an amateur light-heavy weight at the time. Eventually he turned professional, his debut being at York Hall in early September 1996 which he won by stoppage in round two. My job gave me access to the entirety of the venue and after the bout I went to his dressing room and said a quick "well done:'

It became a regular thing throughout Dom's career. I saw all but one of his fights, the other being at Bristol. Even if I wasn't working, I made a point of being there as a boxing fan because in a somewhat strange way I loved his aggressive no fear attitude.

After only five contests Dom was given a shot at the Southern Area Cruiserweight title held by Tottenham boxer Chris Henry. It was a bout which in my opinion should never have been allowed because although Dom won by a 10th round stoppage neither he nor his opponent (who had only six contests, lost two) had gone beyond six rounds. It turned out to be a hard demanding fight between two virtual novice pros and ended with Henry suffering serious injuries and never boxed again.

Although initially ecstatic at his victory, I know Dom suffered emotionally for some while afterwards. Yet, the hard man that he is, he twice went to the hospital to see his stricken opponent, but each time couldn't bring himself to actually enter the building. That was sheer emotion, but demonstrated the kind, thoughtful side of his character whilst mainly hidden from the outside world. I know this because in subsequent conversations, Dom told me openly just how badly he had felt.

Yet he regrouped and his career moved on and for a while most of his bouts were scheduled for 10 rounds. He lost his Southern Area title, regained it and lost it again, and even had a British Title eliminator.

His career eventually finished on a questionable note in July 2002 following a fight against touted Olympic gold medal winner Audley Harrison. In round five of a six rounder Dom was pushed to the canvas, but before he got up Harrison took a blatant liberty landing a punch to his head. Incensed Dom leapt to his feet, offered remarks before nutting his opponent. It was a natural reaction to his violent personality.

Only the excellent action of the referee prevented a possible riot. Dom had sold over 600 tickets mostly in the East End. He should have been disqualified for his action, but instead was allowed to continue only to lose the six rounds decision. The subsequent aftermath has been well documented and therefore requires no further comment from me.

Although his boxing career was over, I saw Dom on a regular basis as he continued to work for the main security firm policing professional boxing shows.

We also had quite frequent telephone conversations albeit I rarely got hold of him because he seemed to changed his mobile phones regularly for reasons best known to himself!!

There was a time when he had some lady problems amongst other things and wanted to chat so I agreed to meet him one evening at a pub in Epping. At the time I was seeing a lady who was the Human Resource Director of a large well know charity company. She decided that she wanted to meet this "interesting character" therefore came with me.

We spent a couple of hours together with Dom revealing his tales of woe. At one time my lady needed to "powder her nose" and whilst she was away Dom remarked "fucking hell mate, you're a bit out of your league there aren't. you?". "What do you mean?", I asked, "well she's all posh like, what does she want to meet me for?" Her return brought that part of the conversation to a close.

During that period of time Dom was apparently due to attend something in Potters Bar, close to where I live. He called me and asked "is it okay to crash out at your place for a few nights?". Luckily my lady friend was staying with me so I told him it wasn't possible. Added to that I didn't fancy the prospect of the Old Bill kicking my front door in at about 4am in the morning. It may not have happened but the thought did cross my mind. I knew Dom was sailing seriously close to the wind, but in some respects I believe lady luck helped him out!

A violent man certainly in his younger days, he has always had a softer, kinder side to his personality.

Although we haven't had much contact in recent years I remember a lot about him and always maintained a soft spot.

I know if I ever had a major problem apart from health, he would be there for me.

Although I have great respect and affection for Dom, I would always regard him as a rascal, a loveable rogue.

RON LEWIS
(R.I.P 2023 – Journalist)

I know Dom through the boxing scene. I was about 17/18 years old at the time. He had his professional career, when he fought Audley and he was involved with some fights after that.

I saw him a lot after that doing the security at a lot of the fights. We would always have a nice chat and he was very good company and that's really how I know him. With the security, when there was a fight in the crowd, he would often be the first man up there and you know, sometimes the fighting crowds would scatter when he got there, because I don't suppose he is anyone you would want to mix with in those situations.

"I can say anything I want?? Lol, but not sure I necessarily want it published".

His career wasn't that great, and his most famous fight is remembered for him head butting Audley Harrison. He didn't have any pretence about his boxing ability and was always honest and a great trier. You know he was not someone I would imagine ever holding a grudge outside the ring.

At the same time, he is not someone you would ever say, or I don't think anyone would ever say "You're a bum" or that sort of shit,

Dom was always a very, in a way he was almost a too open sort of guy. He was always sort of lovely, you know. He has this openness with people and willingness to talk and you know when Dom asks "how's the family?" it is a genuine, sincere question as opposed to a chuck away one.

Bella is roughly the same age as my oldest son, and I would have lots of open talks with him about kids, and you know how it changes your life. The enjoyment they give you and that sort of thing and how special they make you feel.

You wouldn't normally have those conversations as a journalist with a boxer or ex-boxer, but he was just a friendly, open, loveable character and that's what sticks in my mind about Dom.

I know from all the stories that he has been involved in some right old stuff, but at the same time he is not going to drag me in to any of that. He is an absolutely straight up, nice bloke.

HARRY HOLLAND
(Trainer and Actor)

I first met my friend Dominic Negus in the 1990's. I knew about him before because I knew his old amateur club Five Star, Lenny Butcher I think was his old trainer there. So, I knew about him as an amateur boxer, but had never actually met him.

In the 1990's I think Frank Maloney took over managing him as a pro, and I was going over to see Lennox Lewis in Las Vegas and for some reason we had to stay over in San Francisco. It wasn't planned. Dominic Negus was there with a few friends, and we instantly got on straight away and I thought 'what a nice fella'. We just clicked straight away. Dom invited me to come down with him and his friends to the Fisherman Walk which was a famous place in San Francisco. We went to a lovely restaurant there, I remember having a lovely lobster, I don't often have lobster because I can't afford it lol, but it was a lovely lobster, and that was my first night and meeting with Dominic.

I kept an eye on his career and we crossed paths at different times with each other. I remember he boxed Audley Harrison and after got disqualified. He hated Audley after that. What was quite funny was after that I became Audley's Cut man for all his fights and Dom was then a security officer. He used to say to me "How's Ordinary?", as in Ordinary Harrison, we always used to have a laugh.

As far as fighting goes, I feel he never reached his full potential. I wished I had managed him and that's the truth. At the time I was doing quite well with me boxers, and I wished I had managed him.

After that my son used to have some boxing shows and Dom would come and do the security for us, as we were friends.

What I love about him is I like people, and so does he, and he has got respect for older people, how he treats people. He is a perfect gentleman. I find him a complete and utter lovely great fella. But, if you upset him, that's it. I love that sort of person, that's a real man, and Dominic Negus is a real man. He has got a great sense of humour, and everyone I know has never had a bad word to say about him.

Anytime he needed any help, I would be there for him. He is an utter gentleman. Tough man in the ring, tough man out the ring, but a gentleman to go with it.

BARRY JONES
(Ex Boxing Champion and TV Boxing
Commentator/Pundit)

Boxing, for people who have done it, it saves your life. We have all come from difficult backgrounds. Some people come from a bad background and have a bad life and some people like me come from a bad background and have got away from it. I came from a shitty council estate in Cardiff, but I never lived any part of that life. I was around it but somehow avoided it. I didn't look to, but somehow did. My brother didn't, but I know what it's like to be around it.

I found sport from a young age.

Dom finished his career after the Audley Harrison fight which was of course a bit of a spectacle in itself. Boxing is a funny sport, you are family at one time but it can chew you up and spit you out. If Dom had been more dedicated he could have been a lot better boxer than he was.

After that he was the one that would always look after us all. All the TV guys would be on their way to the venues, Dom would be the big friendly bear, which I am sure he has been called that before I would imagine. He was the one that always looked after you. He is just the loveliest guy.

Boxing can be full of scum bags, but even though I have known Dom's background and have heard third party stories of his chequered past and the things he has got up to, we never saw that.

I remember someone was having a go at me once. I think it might have been the Copper Box or Wembley Arena, and doing my job as a commentator. Family members of the boxers who have fought and lost sometimes would wanna put their opinion towards you in not a very flattering manner. You know people calling you names. If 5ft 6 and a half and a former Super Featherweight boxer, I'm a small guy. I have people shouting and getting abusive at me.

In a commentating team there is an ex-boxer, that's what I was. I was a former World Champion and then there is the proper commentator, the journalist who prints the story. I give the technical input. But it's what I say that gets noticed, so if I think you are winning or losing a fight or saying you are doing this or that wrong, people will take it as a positive or negative, boxers and their families will take it personal even though I never say anything bad, they will take it the wrong way.

Anyway, this one time I remember this guy and his wife were having a real go at me saying "you don't know what you are going on about. You're a fucking wanker" and all this stuff. I am just sitting there ringside, not scared, but like "what the fuck have I done here?". I didn't even know whose family it was.

Dominic has the friendliest face in the world and the nicest manner and he comes across, without making him sound thick, just as the friendliest and dopiest guy without a care in the world.

Without asking, he must have heard or seen what was going on, Dom just walked over, with a big smile on his face, put his hand on the guy's shoulder, said something to the both of them. I never asked him what he said. He was smiling, but his eyes were different. I'm not sure what that means, I can't even put my finger on it. He didn't charge over to them, if anything I would love to say he just floated over. He didn't use his hands or point his fingers. He just walked over. His mouth was smiling but his eyes were saying, I'll put you in a fucking bag in a minute. He might have even said that to them lol, but I never asked. All I was thinking was thank fuck Dom is here, otherwise I would have had that in my ear all night, people shouting at me. I still wonder what he said to them as they literally shut up and walked away.

Dom literally used to pick me up and walk me to behind the scenes, to a safe place. It was his job to make sure that no one fucking has a go at you, in any shape or form. I always seemed to gravitate towards him, even though there are loads of security there, everyone knows Dom, the safest place to be is with him. He's a big bloke, he is not the biggest bloke on the planet but you just know you are safe with him. On the ground, where I work, you knew with Dom being there you were in a safe place. Without him ever having to boast or show it, his strength or his menacing side, he didn't have to show it. People knew it, people that knew him knew it, the public knew it. He would just walk around with a smile and having a laugh, he somehow had a way that you just knew. You also knew you couldn't upset him.

As you get with a lot of people who have a chequered past and could be quite dangerous, they don't mention anything. He has an aura about him, even though I have never seen anything but a nice side of him. I don't know real stories, I have just heard rumours. As I said I don't know and it's not my place to say either, but he has never, ever mentioned anything. I know he has had documentaries and that, but he never mentions anything. He doesn't talk about himself in that way.

I just know him as being a lovely guy. Ultimately, he is just a nice guy to be around. As I said, I only know him from the boxing and I don't know him that well, but he is a guy I always want to hug when I see him. I'm not from the generation where I pretend that everyone is a part of my family, or best mates with everybody, but there is something about him. People like him are far and few between to be honest. He is always polite and friendly. You know like they put a smile on your face just for being there. There are not many people like that and as I said I don't know Dom really well, but he does that for me. He makes me feel happy and safe.

I think if ever anything happens to me, he would be the one to step up.

JOHN RAWLING
(TV Boxing Commentator)

I know Dom through the boxing from the late 1990's. He appeared on various undercards on which I commented and was involved in. He was known as a bit or a hard lad and a handful. I didn't think he was ever going to be propelled into the top end of boxing. There are journeymen in boxing and Dom was definitely more than that. He was a strong man who was going to give a good fight as he did with Audley. As far as boxing goes, he was a tough kid.

In the ensuing years when I saw him as a boxer, a trainer and as security, I was always very very pleased to see him. He was a gentleman. He genuinely was and I am a big believer in first impressions and Dom to me was this. He was genuine, respectful, friendly, open and very pleasant to be around.

As security Dom always made sure we were ok at ringside. When you are working ringside you know that professionally you are a target. There are idiots out there who want to be tough, many of whom that are not tough at all. It was reassuring that someone like Dom had my back.

He was there one day over in Belfast at the Ulster Hall where there was a big fight. I can't remember who was fighting. It was a Protestant guy versus a Catholic guy. We felt vulnerable. Dom was there working the security and it was really great knowing that he was behind me looking after my well-being.

When you have a microphone in your hand you are not too aware of what is going on behind you. If it starts to kick off in the crowd it is potentially a fairly scary situation. Knowing Dom was there looking after the security and making sure all is ok. That is very very reassuring.

I know I mentioned one occasion, but he has done this for us many many times. He was involved in the security in the inner ring if you like, where we were commentating and trying to do our bit as well as we could.

When Dom has worked as a trainer with the young fighters, I have seen the way he has been with them. Similarly, he has been nothing but kind and supportive with them. He has tried to let them achieve something within the sport which he has had a long relationship with. I love seeing anybody that cares and has a passion and Dom is definitely one of those.

I don't have colourful stories about Dom, obviously he knows how to handle himself. I know what he did in the past and what he was involved in but that didn't cut across my world.

I always thought the man was an absolute diamond. I have a lot of time for Dom. As far as I am concerned, as I said you take as you find people. I don't care about what people say about reputations and all of it, I want to make my own opinion. And I always thought of Dom from the very first time I met him, right the way through to now was a thoroughly genuine human being whose company I enjoyed.

I always found him a pleasant guy to deal with and as the decades have passed since then, I always like to see him. He always has a smile and is one of those people that when you meet him you think yeah life is better for knowing people like him.

I remember he once said to me and please don't take this the wrong way, "if there is anything that you are in trouble with in your life, and you need somebody to give you a bit of help". I mean, I know what he is saying, like if anybody is threatening you and you need a bit of muscle to back you up, he said "I'll be there for you". That might sound wrong in print and I don't want it to sound that way, but, from my prospective as a journalist and commentator, who is passing judgement on fighters or people who have a very very committed fan base, to know there is someone who says if you get into any kind of trouble I will be there for you, is comforting.

I have always found Dom kind, supportive and caring and when he has had anything to do with me very very engaging, warm and just a genuinely nice man. Anyone who has seen anything other than this, it is not a side that I have seen. And, ok, I don't mix in the circles that Dom once upon a time did.

I respect and like Dom very much and hopefully he likes me too.

MICHAEL PASS
(Boxing Compere)

I have known Dom really since the tail end of his professional boxing career, about 1999/2000, he must have been pushing 30, then he went onto the unlicensed circuit. He went quite far in boxing. I think his cards he was fighting were on rival promoters so I never had the pleasure of announcing him.

I knew him as a boxing ring bouncer at the time, I was working for Sky TV, ITV, BBC, Channel 4. He tended to be at all of the promotions as security, and that is really where I know Dom from, the security side of things.

I had seen the documentaries about him and I have read his first book, and paid full price for it, so he knows I like him.

He always and I don't know if he does it with other people, but he as always called me by my surname, Mr Pass. That to me was always a calming influence because these shows were huge on occasions, going out live on ITV to six to seven million viewers, and my nerves could jangle. What I remember about Dom was that he was always one of the first people I saw because he wouldn't let you in unless you had the proper credentials, as being head of security.

As I approached the arena even though I had been at the game for quite a few years and done some big fights, I was terribly nervous even though it would never show and even reflecting on it now makes me nervous. I could brim with confidence when it was actually live, when I used to enter the ring it was different. I think Dom could always gauge I was edgy, but unlike other people I would talk to on the night, Dom would talk about our children, his daughter Annabella had just been born or was one or two. And through the early infancy of his daughter's life, myself and him would just talk about our respective daughters.

My daughter is about three years older and we would really engage in conversation about them. We would talk for over 20 minutes, even an hour. It was never about boxing, never about outside influences, it was always about our children. He always had a great big smile when he spoke about her. I always respected him for that.

He was always really good on shows.

I won't name names on the next story. Dom loves the guy, I can't stand him, but that is friendships for you. We were up in Newcastle once, I can't remember what the card was it was about 2002. The show had finished and there was about 20 of us back in the hotel, just relaxing having a beer, having a wine, just totally relaxing. Dom had finished his duties for the night and was with a few other security guards. There was the Chairman of the British Boxing Board of Control with us and quite a few high dignitaries and we were all just sat there.

128

I had this reputation in boxing of being a tight Northerner, in fact they used to call me "How Much?" That's what I would say to any price issue lol. It came to my round and I was dreading it. I am used to a round of two or three people, if it had just been Dom I would have bought him a drink no problem. There was about 20 of us.

There was one guy I didn't want to buy a drink for, but thought I had better buy him a drink as it would look odd if I don't, and people would know, as people always knew there was an edge between me and him. Dom specifically knew about this edge to the fact that he was sitting close to me and him that night lol. Poor Dom was switched off for the night, but he was still switched on. I went up to the guy and said "I am getting a round in, what do you want? you drink a large wine don't you?". Even back then a large wine was double figures and I was thinking Christ I could get about five beers for that at home. He was like "I don't want an F***ing drink off you".

Thought fair enough, but still went to the bar and thought the right thing to do was to still get him a drink. I came back gave him his drink which he proceeded to throw over me!!!! I thought what a f*** ing waste of money. I jumped up straight away and this guy I was going for was a pretty handy guy, but when tempers flared, you know it's strange what happens to men You will hit anybody. I went for him straight away, but as I stood up from the chair Dominic was right in front of me "Mr Pass, Mr Pass you know you don't want to do it". It was just a brilliant calm influence, once again. I can't commend him enough. That night he was my guardian angel because we could have all lost our licences. I don't even remember Dom getting up. All I remember like the second coming of Christ which hasn't come yet, he was just there in front of us, massive smile and just completely, completely relaxed. I have never known a guy for it. Honestly.

The following night we were all in Cardiff. The majority of us were working two nights back-to-back and this was the biggest show. The big Joe Calzaghe fight, it was at the Principality Stadium, 80,000 capacity. Everybody that was working on the show knew about the incident obviously, a glass of wine being thrown over me. Dom came up to me in stitches and kept saying to me "I can't believe you paid over 10 quid for a glass of wine for someone who then throws it back over you for buying them a drink". He just found everything quite entertaining.

When we reconnected, I was made up. How we got back in touch was I was driving down to London on a driving assignment and we were stuck in traffic. My colleague said "let's ring some folk from boxing who we haven't spoken to for years". Dom was one of them. I didn't know my colleague was phoning him, it just came out of the blue and it was just great to hear from him.

Don't criticise, don't condemn and don't complain these qualities only come with a powerful person and Dom has these remarkable qualities. I have never seen over those years him do any of those as I said which I find remarkable, especially when you are in the firing line working for all the top boxing promoters in security.

I adore him.

GARY LOCKETT
(Welsh Former Middleweight World Title Challenger)

I had heard of Dominic Negus. It was because of the violent ex life and the boxing. I saw him put the head into Audley Harrison when they fought.

I can remember when I was boxing and he was a pro at the same time, I think we are similar ages, I am 45. I had always heard his reputation as a violent, nasty man, but when I actually met him that was quite the opposite.

Predominantly I know Dom through him being the security for the Frank Warren bills, so, as a trainer I always had boys fighting on the bills.

I always had a reputation as being very steely faced, face down to the ground type of thing and Dom always took the mickey out of me. We always got on and I have always found him as a big friendly giant to be honest. He said I never used to smile and I was a moody git. I started looking at myself when I was on the tv and thought "shit - people have got a point" lol. It looks like I never smile and I'm a right miserable sod, but that's not the case.

In the gym we are always laughing and in my family life we are always happy. I think it is just a persona I am giving off, but I really don't even know that I am doing it.

There is not really a great deal of words I can say, except we have known each other for a substantial amount of time. When we bump into each other at shows, we are always friendly. I can't and haven't seen the violent side to him. He is always just a big friendly giant. We always have a laugh and I still owe him a pint of Guinness.

We always have a good laugh and mess about together and I have never seen anything other than a respectable, old school guy, who is always very friendly.

It is very rewarding and an honour to be asked to say some words. I feel very flattered that Dom thinks that I am a man of respect to have been asked to say something for his book.

MICKY COVENEY
(Former Top Fighter)

I have known Dominic for about 22 years.

I turned professional when I was 18 and am now 40. I remember I first saw Dominic when I walked into, I think it was, a Lennox Lewis gym in about the year 2001 or something like that and he was sparring. He was always larger than life, funny and a good fighter as well.

I remember him fighting Audley Harrison and always holding his own in all his fights. I then used to see him at gyms and shows.

He has a massive personality, big smile, always comes up and gives me a big cuddle. He is a top top top bloke, he is a lovely man and a good fighter.

All I can say about Dominic is, he is one in one, a lovely fella, he means well, he wears his heart on his sleeve and he just a top man, a top bloke.

Everyone likes him. Everyone has got time for him. All I can say he is a top bloke and everyone likes him and of course Dominic is Dominic. He has a big smile, big heart. I can't say enough good things about him.

NICKY THURBUN
(Former British Title Challenger Light/Middleweight)

I met Dominic really from day one in our boxing careers, we both were at the Garden City boxing club back in 1984. I was 11/12 years old.

I walked into the boxing club which was in Hainault, Dom was already a member there he had probably been there a few months before I was. I always remember going in there he came up to me and I said "I've only just started" and he said do you want to have a move around like sparring and I was like "oh no its only my first time" and that is how we met.

I always remember Dominic being an ultra-confident guy, always come up and spoke to you, always friendly and we went through our boxing careers side by side really.

We started at the Garden City Club where Johnny Kingsley trained us, and we both had successful amateur careers. Dom then went off to be with Lennard Butcher over at Five Star, which is where he done most of his amateur boxing and he done very well.

We then progressed into the professionals together, not always the same management but we have always been close friends in the boxing world. We both won Southern Area titles. Both got to a level of sort of British title round that level and obviously Dominic progressed very well in the unlicensed boxing. He was sort of unbeat with the fights he had in that.

Always full of life Dominic. I always loved seeing him as he used to give me so much confidence and he was always bursting with confidence – he always believed in himself and we went on from that.

Since Dominic has come out of the professional boxing he has done a lot of charity work and a lot of unlicensed work in the boxing world, and I refereed him. I'm now doing a lot of boxing refereeing. I refereed Dom's comeback for a charity boxing show.

It's always great to see Dom. He is a great guy and you know a very close friend of mine.

Dom has never ever feared anyone he has always been so confident and that's why everything you do in life is to do with the mind. He has a very very strong mindset, although I know he has had problems with different things in the past, depression and things like that but he never used to come across like that. He was always so confident. He is a very strong bloke, always trained well.

He has put on a bit of weight now but he has always loved fighting, loved boxing. He is a great guy. I have such fond memories of us really.

It is always great to hear from him and as I said although we don't see each other on a regular basis it is so good to see him when I do.

KEVIN MITCHELL
(Former World Lightweight Challenger)

As a kid Dom always inspired me to get into boxing.
He always had time for everyone and always spoke to me and all the other kids too.

My favourite memory was when I was a youngster Dom used to take me backstage with him.

EDDIE LAM
(Trainer and Former Amateur International Boxer)

I have known Dom since the mid 1990's. We boxed around the London amateur circuit together. We were both quite good and rated in the top 10 in the country at the time. He used to box at Five Star in Harold Hill, Romford and I was boxing for the South London Club, Fitzroy Lodge in Lambeth.

He was like a gentle giant really was Dom. I had heard a lot of other stuff and stories about him, but I would never have believed it. When we met he always always nice and warm to me, one of the nicest people I have met.

After our boxing days, I would see him regularly on the circuit as a coach or security guard and he was always a very good friend to me.

I remember seeing him on a tv programme about gangsters and I couldn't believe what I was watching because he wasn't the Dom that I knew. I have never seen that side of him. I guess everyone has to make a living. But that was completely different to the person I knew.

JOHNNY GREAVES
(Top British Journeyman)

Me and Dominic go back quite a good few years now. Well before I turned professional as a boxer myself. I used to fight on the unlicensed scene.

Although I fought for one or two other promoters over the years, the bulk of my work came through Alan Mortlock whose shows were predominantly held at the Circus Tavern in Purfleet in Essex. I aways had hard fights that pleased the crowd. Dom did quite a few fights there, but was also part of the security team.

I was always a big boxing fan and Dom was a face I always kept my eyes on due to him being a London/Essex pro fighter.

Me and Dom got talking over time and I was chuffed with that.

There was a couple of occasions we travelled up to Wales and wot not. We'd get in the minibus, me, Dom, a few other fighters and trainers. I always had a few cans and conversation was lively.

After having 50 unlicensed fights for a few different promoters, I turned Pro. I was already nearly 30 so decided to go pro as a journeyman. A paid opponent as such. Have gloves, will travel, lose, get paid, fight again next week. I was good at my job. After a short time, I was already fighting on big Frank Warren bills.

Dom was working as a main security man on these big world title shows and I got offered a fight on a big promotion in Scotland, Glasgow I think.

I always travelled alone, so after being taken to my hotel I looked around looking for a familiar face or somewhere I could have a beer later.

Anyway, after mooching about all day waiting to fight, I get to the venue and after a while do my thing. After the show I walked into the bar on my jax, pocket full of cash, I thought "fuck it, I'm getting on the lash". Then I spotted Dom and a couple of the other security boys. I really went large and ended up on the piss till silly o'clock, forgetting my pick up from the hotel for our flight home was early morning. I was smashed.

It wasn't until I heard Dom coming through my room door at six or seven in the morning. I started to realise what I'd done.

When you've got a fella Doms size and demeaner screaming at you from the end of your hotel bed, hungover to fuck, you liven up sharpish.

If I missed that plane not only would work have been a bit pissed off, my missus would have killed me. I owe Dom my life on that account HaHa.

Dominic Negus you saved my life. I love you brother

KEN BOXFIT
(Owner Boxfit Boxing Equipment and Customised Clothing)

We have a team of people at Boxfit UK that know Dom through our boxing store and boxing shows that Dom has fought on. Boxfit UK are a supplier of boxing equipment and custom made fight wear and we have supplied Dom with his equipment and custom made fight shorts for many years now. This is how we have built up a friendship with him.

There are so many stories and most of the stories would encapsulate Dom's colourful side. When he enters our

135

store you know you are going to end up belly laughing or cringing with what he is going to get up to and say, but we wouldn't have it any other way.

Even though Dom is a big character and a big guy, you know when you meet up that you are always going to get the biggest embrace and cuddle from him and trust us it will be the biggest bear hug ever!!

137

TRUE RESPECT

"Men of Morals"

JASON GUIVER
(Entrepreneur and Close Friend)

He is a big old minge for a start, laughs, and you can tell him I said that.

We have been mates for ages, years. I used to go and watch Dom when he was a pro.

A funny story, we was training for a fight once, and I went up to his old gym Five Star up in Havering, I believe it was an old amateur gym and where he turned pro out of. I was the Super Cruiserweight unlicensed champion at the time. I think it was about 2003.

Dom had just come off of the pro circuit onto the unlicensed circuit and I picked him up. We went over to the gym, got ready for sparring. We started sparring, I caught him with a couple of good shots, and he didn't like that. So, he hit me round the rib cage and broke three of me ribs.

He actually dropped me off to the hospital, and then he pissed off for three days in me 50 grand car. I was left in bed with broken ribs and didn't know where me car was. My ribs are still bad now, especially in the winter, I'm in agony. They actually stick out.

He was a very very good fighter, even now, if he hits ya you are going to sleep. I have been on the end of them.

When he come off the pro circuit he came onto my association I was fighting on. He was obviously heavyweight. I don't think I would have wanted to have a fight with him in the ring anyway to be honest with you.

I have always been there for Dom, if he has had any trouble, you know what I mean. I have always stood by his side if he's needed it. I know he has got a lot of friends that talk the talk but certainly don't walk the walk in my eyes.

Me and Dom have gone through a lot of things together. Mental health, I suffer from that as well, there is nothing to be ashamed of. I have seen Dom at his lowest and I have seen him at his naughtiest.

Dom, if you really know Dom he is a lovely fella. He is a nice bloke. He went through that stage where he got involved with the wrong people, but I don't believe that was really Dom. I think it was the people that he was with. I'm not really sure what the words are for it, but maybe it brought the worst out in him. Maybe he was trying to be something he really wasn't made for.

But if there is one thing I think Dominic was made for it is fighting.

IAIN MCCALISTER
(CEO MAN Commercial Security)

I have known Dom for well over 25 years, I was thinking about this recently. Back in the day when I first knew Dom he worked for a security company down in London called Top Guard, which was based in Loughton in Essex. I did some work with him in the early 90's and I got to know Dom from about 1999 all the way through to the last couple of years where he worked with my good self and my company MAN Commercial Protection. A lot of the work we have done over the years has been to do with music and sport security.

Predominantly the boxing, obviously the sort of stuff that people see on the tv and Dom he did some of the big shows with us, Joe Calzaghe, Ricky Hatton, David Haye. All the big big shows. Dom was a big part of that.

Not only is he somebody I have known for a long time, but he is a good pal as well. He is very very popular. I think the thing with Dom is he doesn't realise sometimes how popular he is.

He does get a little bit emotional sometimes. He recently texted me about some bits for his daughter as she was looking at universities, which is mad because I remember when she was born and now she is going uni, so it's been a long time. I said to Dom if she is end up going to Birmingham uni, to give her my number and I'll meet up with her, because at the end of the day he is me pal.

I remember we did a show years ago. Dom come up. It was when Amir Khan, who was from Bolton, was making a name for himself and they put this show on at Bolton Arena, which was a man-made arena. They had an outside bar area and it was a real lively show.

With boxing sometimes you get lively and sometimes quiet ones, but this one was lively. There was an issue in the crowd and some of the guys were escorting a fella out and this guy was being a real pain and causing issues, blah blah blah. The guys were so professional and took them what seemed like ages to escort him out of the crowd to an area to get him out. It was funny because it took ages and they were trying to escort him out slowly to cause the least fuss as possible. Anyway, when they got him to the area Dom was standing there lol, and Dom just grabbed him by the throat, lifted him up and just marched him and fired him out the door within five seconds.

It was hilarious really how it started to how it finished really. The fella thought he was doing well until Dom got hold of him. It was funny because it was something that was so different.

I have done shows all over the UK with him that's Scotland, Ireland, England, Wales, I remember doing shows with him in Belfast, Glasgow, Cardiff. I have done dozens and dozens of shows and music shows and he really is very popular. He is so popular, even with me office staff and all that, they all think a lot of him and all that. He is just a big character.

He is so respectful. I have never, ever, ever, not once ever, and I have done hundreds of shows with him, I have never ever ever seen him take liberties. He has never ever. He is the opposite to a bully and the opposite to what I've seen him back in the day when he did those tv shows. They are not a great character of him as he is not like that. He is loyal 100%, and trustworthy.

Dominic with Kevin Mitchell, who he beat in 1999 to win the vacant British Light-heavyweight title

With Mike Bisping, Joe Long and 'Big John'

With Karen Appleton

With Paul, Steve, Tony, Stan, Jo and George

With Alfie Warren

With Stella & Freddy Negus

Dominic relaxing

With Bella, Micky Theo and Lee Matthews

With Mark Potter

With Jason Burton, Jay Cod, Jonno Croney and Freddy Negus

Sanjay, Lyle Gornall, Hamzah and Martin Spicer

With Dean, Rosie and 'Big Chris'

With Lyle Gornall and Stuart Potaznick

Chris Glover

Bob Kipps and Ian Wilson

With Rob Warren

With Jonny, Henry, 'Big H', Martin and James

With Lyle Gornal, Stuart Potaznick and Butch Goldhawk

With Craig, 'Big Chris', Liam and Connor

Dominic and Bella

Dom at the end of the day if he comes to a show 99% of people whether it's the punters or the staff they all know him and are all friendly and ready to have a crack with him.

What I will say is that not many people really know him, they just see his persona, or they just think they see what he is about, but he is loyal. The great thing with loyalty is you can't buy that. He is proper old school.

I know with his reputation and with everything else over many years a lot of people have known him and speak highly of him and all that, but the one good thing about him which I would say is if he is a friend, he is a friend.

If I was coming to Essex at the weekend I would give him a call and he would do the same if he was coming up. We live a couple of hours apart. Every week or every fortnight he will send me a direct message on Facebook or WhatsApp. At the end of the day, you just know you can rely on him. He is just one of them.

When he came back and did his white collar boxing, I come quite a few times to see him. He knows at the end of the day if I said to him I will meet him Sunday, he knows I will meet him and that's likewise. If I was to ring him today, and said I need some help, I know he would be there. With good pals you don't have to be on the phone to them all the time. You just know.

My missus, my daughter, my sons they think a lot of him. You know what you get with Dom and that is exactly it. You know what you get and at the end of the day some people probably think they do know him. I know in the past he said it was tough as some people took the mick about or whatever, but he knows his good pals. He knows them back to front and he knows the people he can trust as well.

Most of them are probably in this book. People like Steve Bunce and all that who have done well for themselves, they will and always have a lot of time for him, that's a big thing really.

Some people have a big aura, a big presence so people leave them alone or kind of keep out of the way of them or maybe they are not sure with them or whatever, but as I say never in my whole life have I ever seen him once turn, he is not like that.

He is one of them you could trust.

DENNIS HOBSON
(Boxing Promoter)

I'd describe Dom as "a proper man".
I think he was training as a pro with Howard Rainey and he introduced us.

We hit it off from then.
Love the man to bits.
A proper dad as well

JOE EGAN
(Former Top International Irish Heavyweight Champion and Former Mike Tyson Sparring Partner)

Dominic Negus is a man I class as a very close friend. Also, a man I hold in very high regard. A man that acquitted himself well in the boxing ring and also was very capable outside the boxing ring.

He is a man of courage and still is a man of courage, and that is something you are born with.

You can give a man the skills to fight, but if he doesn't have the courage to fight then he is no good. You are born with courage. Dominic Negus is a man that was born with an abundance of courage.

One story that springs to mind about courage. The two times Heavyweight Champion of the World, Tony Tucker, was over in the UK doing some boxing matches. Now this man had dominated the world as a world amateur champion and ruled the world as professional. 12 rounds with Mike Tyson, 12 rounds with Lennox Lewis, a phenomenal fighter. So, they have got him over to do boxing matches in the UK. They have got a fight lined up for him in and around London and they were struggling to get a man to fight.

Dominic, who was part of the security, looking after the man, said "I'll give him a fight". Dominic boxed at a good level in the UK but now he is on the stage with the two times world heavyweight champion in the world and he got in, no problem. Dominic got in and gave a great account of himself. I think it was a six round fight and Dominic was in there for every round for six rounds. So, I admire the man to jump in with the two times Heavyweight Champion of the World and didn't even bat an eyelid with the opposition when the opportunity came up. So that's just one of the stories of a man of courage.

Another story I remember was The Kostya Tszyu / Ricky Hatton fight in Manchester. My two brothers, one came over from Canada, and one came over from Belfast and they phoned me and said they had bought three tickets for the fight. I said "what did you buy tickets for?" They said "it's gonna be so hard to get in, it's sold out". They said "we are very very lucky to get three tickets together"". I said my friend, Ian Mccallister does all the security and I said Dominic Negus is his head of security - they are my pals - I would have been able to get us in". My brothers said "we can't and won't take that chance". Anyway, we went and we were sitting high up in the gods. To see the boxing ring you needed binoculars, but that was my two brothers.

Anyway, on the evening of the show I get a phone call from Mark Peters and Mick Cooke. Mark was a compere and Mick another bodyguard. They phone me to say "Joe is there any chance you might be able to get us into the show, we have had no luck with ticket touts and all the tickets are sold out and we want to be there". I said let me see what I can do and I phone Dominic. Dominic said "no problem Joe" As quick as that, "tell them to get round to gate 13 and I'll look after them." Fair play to Dominic.

I am sitting up in the gods, needing binoculars to see the ring. I phoned Mick and said go to gate 13 and Dominic will look after you. Well, they phoned me and said Joe "thank you so so much, Dominic has brought us in, we are sitting ringside next to Russel Crowe and Prince Naseem". I could have strangled my two brothers lol. There's me up

143

high struggling to see. I am looking down with my binoculars and they are waving up at me, having got in for free with Dominic, ringside. Fair play to Dominic he did me proud with me two pals.

He is a kind man as well. All rolled into a big bundle of joy. He is a good man and I'm not saying it because he is my friend.

GLYN RHODES MBE
(Former Boxer and Gym Owner)

I have known Dominic for what seems like forever. I can't tell you exactly when I first met him, I think the 1990's, but it's been a long long time. We bump into each other at shows up and down the country on a regular basis. He is a big friendly giant. He is a big character. Everyone knows he is a big character.

Like I said we see each other at the boxing shows and he is just a great kid. He is everything he doesn't appear to be, if you know what I mean. He looks like a big aggressive type, but he is everything but that and once you get to know him he is not that at all.

So many stories, all mainly from boxing shows. He once stopped me having a go at someone should I say. I had a bit of a fall out with someone at a boxing show which is nothing new for me, always falling out with somebody and Dominic was the one who picked me up off the floor and told me to calm down, which I'm glad he did, and we've friends ever since.

Picture this. We were in the Midlands hotel in Manchester. George Forman the former Heavyweight Champion was at the hotel, for the Nazeem Hamed fight. You had Tommy Hearns and Emmanuel Steward playing pool and Dominic is obviously doing the security trying to stop people from getting in. It was a surreal picture.

There is a kid in the gym called Fraser, a lovely kid. He has a few issues and has been coming to the gym since he was five, he is 19 now. Through my association with Dominic on Facebook and with Fraser liking Dom's post he one day came to the gym and said "I have requested Dominic as a friend on Facebook and he has accepted it". Through this they have become quite friendly and Dominic loves him to bits.

Recently Dominic said he was coming past Sheffield and he was gonna pop in. So, I said to Fraser the Razor, that's what he call him, that Dominic's coming to the gym and are you able to get here. He was so excited that he was actually going to be able to meet Dominic in person.

On the day he nearly never made it as the bus driver drove past Fraser, but luckily one of his mums' friends took him. To be honest I would have paid for a cab for him as he was so excited to finally be able to meet Dom and I would have hated for him to miss that opportunity.

When he walked in and saw Dominic it made his day, mind you Dominic said meeting him made his day and cheered him up too.

As I said, known him for what seems like forever,

Love him to bits.

WAYNE TANK CALVELEY
(Security Consultant)

I met Dom whilst working on security for MAN Commercial Protection. I have worked several festivals with him but mainly boxing shows organised by Frank Warren.

We were working a fight at EXCEL in London and the boxers were staying at a hotel near the venue. Iain McCallister (owner of MAN) said "lads I need you to walk over and get one of the boxers for me and escort them back to the venue!" Dom replied "which boxer is it?" of which Iain replied "It's Audley Harrison". Dom then replied back with raised words "I ain't fucking walking over there to escort him back" (or something along those lines). Due to their fight in 2002.

I also witnessed Dom escorting a group of lads out of a venue during another boxing event. The lads were shouting that we are going to report you to the organiser.

"Tell Frank Warren and tell him I escorted you out. The names NEGUS, that's N.E.G.U.S". Think the lads realised who he was and calmly left the venue not even turning around to have another look.

JIMMY YELLOP
(Friend)

Dom was a really good friend of my dad, they had done work together over the years. Dom is a year older than me. We got on like a house on fire and have been friends ever since. We are not friends really, we are family. He is like a big brother of mine. We have known each other 30 years. I knew him in his early 20's when he was boxing.
My brother-in-law, Terry Foy, was ABA heavyweight boxing champion and he needed a sparring partner. Because all the boxers fight at that weight he couldn't get a sparring partner. So me dad, the big Jimmy Yellop said "I will get Dominic to spa with ya", to get him ready for the ABA finals in York Hall, Bethnal Green.

I mentioned it to Terry and he was like "oh brilliant". He had heard of Dominic because Dom was a pro fighter and he, Terry, was an amateur at the time. We spoke with Dominic and arranged to meet at Changs Night Club in Walthamstow.

He was a bit sceptical, but I said Dom is a pal of mine and he's not a problem. He had heard about Dom's reputation. I was like he is absolutely like family to us. Me and my dad wouldn't do that to you.

We went and I introduced him to Dominic. We had a couple of drinks. A couple of people came in and I'm not sure if they owed him money or had done something wrong to Dom. Dom said to Terry "Would you mind holding my drink for me please?". Dom has turned round and gone to work on them. Smashed them to pieces. The doormen have come up, they have got smashed to pieces by Dom too. Next minute there's five big heavy blokes on the floor and Dom standing over them. He then comes back to us, as cool as a cucumber and says "Tel, can I have

146

my drink back please". He's looked at Terry, looked at me and carried on chatting as if nothing had happened.

As soon as Dom went to the toilet, Terry said to me "I don't think I want to spar with Dom" lol. "In case I catch him with a lucky shot or something he might kill me", haha. They never did spar together, he really was too scared too.

I went to see him at the Audley Harrison fight, what a funny story that is. Maloney was his manager and put the fight together. Audley won the Olympic gold medal. So, the BBC gave him a 10 fight deal, a million pound, 100 grand a fight. I think it was his third fight and offered to fight Dominic who at the time wasn't a heavyweight.

We were all at the press conference and they said "how's it going to go". Frank Maloney, who is now Kellie Maloney said "on paper Audley Harrison should box his head off, because he has just won gold. He is a heavyweight, got a longer reach, got a weight advantage and everything. But if it was in a phone box, Dominic would smash the granny out of him.

After the fight, which Audley won on points, they were interviewing Dominic in a press conference and they said "How do you reckon he will get on with the next seven fights?" and Dom said "Not very good, my mum hits harder than he does". He said "I ain't got a mark on me, she does hit harder than him". That's Dominic all over, quick witted, with a smile on his face.

I love him.

MARK EPSTEIN
(Former MMA Fighter – "The Beast")

The first time we met was quite interesting. This is my first memory.   It was about 2013 I was working for Match Room at the Mecca of British boxing, York Hall, Bethnal Green. I was doing security over there. Dominic had a fighter on the show and was there with quite a few of his supporters. I was working and Dominic was there as a coach for his fighter.

147

The guy I was working with that day, Andy, who is lovely but liked to walk around as if he was the biggest body builder on the planet. He is quite a big guy but walks around as if he is twice the size he is, which is quite funny.

Anyway, he got into some altercation with Dominic and his supporters and I had to go and get involved. It kicked off and Andy was just about to get his arsed handed to him by Dominic and his crew. I have gone over there and got involved.

I knew who Dominic was, what he had been through and of course I had seen numerous programmes about him. I also knew he was a boxer. That's why I had to get involved. Even though Andy was head of security at the time, but he obviously didn't know who Dominic was and what he was about.

I went over and calmed the situation and pulled people apart and got stuck in, without throwing any punches. I was just trying to calm things down. Andy got his shirt ripped off him completely and took a few digs as well. I ain't gonna lie, he is a game fella and gave a few digs too, but I feel like I saved Andy's life, not literally. But, if it was going to go off it would have gone proper pear shaped. He is as game as they come but he definitely bit off more than he could chew. He was definitely going to get a hiding. I'm pleased I intervened when I did and calmed things down.

That was my first real meeting of Dominic. I will never forget that. A very interesting and memorable first meeting. After that incident we got chatting and have been friends since.

Dom is lovely but scary, it depends on the day how you get him. I know in his younger days he was very wild, but as we get older we all mellow.

Ever since then we speak on social media quite a lot and whenever we see each other, we always give each other a big hug.

He is a father and a great father. A loyal friend. One of the type of friends that would be there for you through thick and thin. I know this. I would never ask Dominic to get involved if I had a problem as would not want to put him in that situation, however, I know I could ask him for anything and he would be there for me and vice versa.

I class him as a good friend and I have nothing but the utmost respect for him.

JEREMY BAILEY
(Entrepreneur and Top Promoter)

I first met Dom round about early 2000. I knew of Dom through the boxing first of all because he was high profile. I come from a fighting background as well and we had some mutual friends.

I started putting on shows, doing the promoting for shows and Dom was one of the guys heading up one of the security teams.

My first interaction with him personally was in a show in York Hall, Bethnal Green. Where I had a bit of a past and reputation, I had booked the venue and obviously someone had found out about my past and they had insisted that Dom was there or I couldn't have the show.

I met Dom that night at the show. As I said I knew of him and had heard about him through and following the boxing. We just hit if off first time and it has been the same ever since to be honest.

On the night of my show in York Hall we had an incident in the crowd. Basically, there was a rival fighter and one of their supporters had come along and was being a right arsehole. He ended up starting in the crowd, whacking a girl and throwing a chair. It was really unusual to get that behaviour, especially with anything to do with martial arts.

Anyway, for me, because I knew what was riding on this event for me, and what with my reputation I thought "Oh my god, I can't have this". Once I saw him punch this girl, I made a beeline for him, and as I'm making my way for him, Dom is making his way over there as well.

Dom has managed to get hold of this guy, take him out one of the back exits and I've said to Dom "listen I need to speak to him". Dom was like "no, no, he's leaving. His behaviour is a liberty". You know Dom was being really professional at doing his job, he is very very stringent, and when he says no he means no. Anyway, I have said to him "Dom let him go, just let him go. I just need him for literally 10 seconds" and Dom was like "do you know him?".

As Dom turned round to let him go, I just laid into the guy. I let him have it, I mean completely. I come from a martial arts background, so when I have kicked him to the floor, his teeth have come out. All the security came over to split it up and the woman that was running the venue was going mad. Amongst all the screaming and madness and her shouting all sorts of abuse at me, Dom calmly said to me "I wish more fucking people would be like you".

Dom turned around and said to everyone "shut the fuck up, listen he has done the right thing". Literally everyone shut up and went back to work like it was normal. From that moment me and Dom just hit it off. He was like "fair play to you, you got some bollocks". I was like "why wouldn't I - you don't punch a woman ever and you can't throw chairs in my show, that's just not the way it works." After that we have worked together on various security things where there has been absolute mayhem kicking off. The thing with Dom is that he is a no nonsense, straight to the point, not going around the houses, big scary motherfucker, but he is an absolute gentleman with very very high morals.

I think he just has a massive heart of gold as well. That's the thing with Dom, that's probably the thing I notice the most about him, you know, everyone says how scary he is and the things that he has done, but what an absolute gentleman. For me, and I can honestly say that he has never been anything but straight with me.

There is never a time when you are around Dom that something funny or outrageous doesn't happen. Whether that is a working environment or a personal one.

I will tell you some stories lol. There has been numerous occasions when we have all been out with a few people, all mutual friends around the fight scene and fight world, you know promoters, ex fighters, security guys. I will reiterate we are not looking for trouble when we are out, it's just not what we do. We are not there to give anyone a hard time. We are polite, we are respectful. However, some times the younger generation and the door staff and security guys who haven't come up the ladder the same way we had and might not be fully aware of who is who.

Around 2015 we were in a fairly well-known establishment in Central London, and these guys were trying to give us a hard time. We were like "come on, let's leave it, it's just not worth it". We are looking to go and the security are getting a bit heavy handed with us, and lets just say on that night, I'm not gonna lie, Dom went first as per usual. Dom gave everyone a front row pay for view that they would never have seen anywhere else, believe me.

Basically, between all of us we slumped the whole team, I mean the whole team of floor staff. We just walked out, obviously we finished our drinks and then just walked out.

That was typical of how it was. It's a Dom thing he would be polite and say "listen guys, come on don't be like that, we are not here for any trouble" and then someone would put their hand on him, and that would be it…… Everyone is getting it. I think that's fair play, you can't back down, you have tried to walk away, try to find a positive resolution to it, but someone always tries their luck and takes it too far. The problem is they push and push and push and you tell them that they don't want it and then they complain when they get the reaction.

He is just straight talking like that and I don't think you can fault him for it, you know.

I live out of London and I could be in some kind of madness, whacking some people or whatever and literally I'm not even joking, this has happened a few times, definitely at the 02. Something has kicked off and I have ended up knocking one or two people out and there is pandemonium and I am screaming at security for back up and literally as calm as anything Dom will walk through "hello darling", and I'm like "Oh my god", laughs. He always just turns up and I'm like to everyone it's all good Dom is here and he is like "Alright Jel?". I will tell him what has happened and he will be like "ok", will turn around to

151

the security and say "the problems done, it's all resolved". He just has the ability to do that.

It can all be kicking off, he will turn up with a cheeky little wink or something and you know you are stopping. It is just what it is.

He is just a lovely, lovely guy. Everyone has respect for him. That just sums him up really.

The thing is for me, I have had some crazy nights with Dom where it has all gone off, but honestly and truthfully, hand on heart, some of the best conversations I have had with him will be about our daughters. Just out of the blue he will message me "any joy with your daughter?". That side of him many don't see. Everyone sees the hardman, the athlete, the boss, but not many see the loving father. I have seen that side.

There was a time when we didn't see lots of our daughters, we connected over that, we'd send each other messages and ring each other up, you know, especially on the days when it might be hitting you that little bit harder. That's a real connection to be honest.

Don't get me wrong, we have had our moments that have been fun, but the other side of him I have seen the doting loving father that he is.

It will be wonderful if people got to know about that side of him, as everyone knows about the other side. But I know he is doing his best now to make up for lost time. That was not down to him, you know.

The thing is that people don't understand, it makes you a cold person when your children are not fully in your life. You know, did anyone ever stop to think why was he sometimes the way he was?. Maybe that was his coping mechanism, maybe that was his way of dealing with it. Regardless whether we say it was right, or if someone agrees or disagrees with it, I can say Dom has never been a bully, if anything he stands up for the people being bullied. It is never going to be some shiny bum that Dom has whacked up, it is going to be some other hardman, villain or bully that has picked on someone else and it is Dom sticking up for them. From that side of it, nobody has complaints about him, because he is not out there rolling over shiny bums because that is not what he is about.

Anger can make you a different person and I don't think people always realise that. Sometimes it's just, I don't want to sort of say it's not your fault, but you just don't know any better. You are on auto pilot. At the end of the day anger is an emotion, people say a bad one, but it's not. If you know how to use it, anger can get you through. The thing that people don't realise is, and I know it's going to sound bad, but that sort of thing can be therapy for you. What drives a man to be like this? What goes on in his thoughts when he is on his own?. What keeps him up at night?. What keeps him awake? What drives him?

Dom is a devoted dad and those that know him, know that is exactly what his life is all about, Bella. There are times when he might have wanted to sign out, not wanted to be here, but he is. Bella is the driving force behind that.

JOHN NOVO
(Former Security Consultant)

My memory is not so great. I have forgot about a lot of my past it's true. Its only what people tell me.

However, I do remember I met Dom probably about coming onto about 30 years ago. At the time I was about mid 20's and I was a manager for a security company that he came over to work for, Top Guard. He came to do some work. I was Operational Manager so we did a lot of raves, clubs, events, boxing up and down the country. We even had sub offices in Manchester, Plymouth and Wales. There was loads of people that worked for us.

I remember Dom coming to us he was probably about 18/19 at the time. He was young, very young. Most of us were probably mid 20's, if not older. He was one of the youngest guys ever to come and join us. To be honest, I can't even remember how he came about coming to us. Most of the time people are introduced to us but Dom all I remember, he was very young looking. He looked even younger than his age. He had glasses on, roundish face, big broad smile, really cheeky. He was really keen to do the work and get involved and wanted to be a part of it.

I do remember him getting into boxing and thinking how did he get on with it. It was us that named him The Milky Bar Kid. Because of his age and the character from the advert, I think that was before he got into boxing, or the early days of his training.

Obviously he did events at different venues for us over the years but I actually came away from the industry, I can't quote what year. I got out of it before it came bigger even though it was very big at the time. I stepped away and lost touch with the majority of the people.

I remember back in the day him boxing at Wembley and head butting Audley Harrison.

I had heard through other people over time about the things what Dom had been up to - a colourful life to say the least. Decades had gone past in between and we'd lost contact. I remember seeing him on tv programmes, it was strange as I had stepped away from that life and was leading a different life. So seeing those things on tv I was surprised to see.

I knew he had had a daughter and we started connecting through Facebook. He had the Sparta gym and was doing a lot of training other people. It was so good to see that he had turned his life around and how he has become a different man altogether.

The main thing is I am so pleased how he has ended that other life.

The books have come out and his pod casts. He has turned his life around. His life is all about his Bella now and moving on.

It is good to see that he and some other people we used to know have moved onto better things in life.

I wish him all the best. It still makes me laugh when I see pictures of him as he still has that big smile - it's no different to that 18/19 year old kid that walked into our office in Essex looking for work.

He has never changed, just become a lot bigger - in more ways than one!

JAY ASTLEY (BOD)
(Bodyguard and Close Friend)

For many years me and Dom were well known for working at the Mecca for British boxing, York Hall, Bethnal Green. We were always fair but old school stand up guys. We worked for many promoters in various arts of fighting, kickboxing, amateur boxing, white collar boxing and unlicensed boxing, which we both took part in. But mainly pro boxing which Dom did to a very high standard.

As a fighter, a trainer and of course security we were like a double act, wherever it kicked off, we were there in the blink of an eye.

We weren't troublemakers and never bullies, but we were stand up, old school security protectors.

Every time we spotted a bully we would search for him sometimes leaving York Hall to go to the pub over the road. Well sneaking off over the pub. Our boss and famous pro boxing promoters would ask "where are Dom and Bod?". They'd be getting worried then we would magically appear and someone would be straightened out in the pub toilets. Was it us doing the straightening????? Hmmmmm!!!!

Many years ago, on July 16th 2005 we were doing a show on Sky Sports. A boxing show in Bolton with Amir Khan as the headline fight. There was a lot of trouble in the crowd, all of the trouble seemed to be caused by one man, a big dude in white jeans. This guy was in a fight in the crowd which we split up and escorted him outside. He was a proper stand up dude who was up for it.

An hour later the police were asking where he was by describing him. We said we didn't know, but the rumour was he was asleep in the Biffa bin around the back and when he woke up he was so confused and hadn't a clue how he ended up there ..... And of course, those white jeans were a total mess!!!!!

We still believe in one on one straighteners in car parks with one person with you so it doesn't get out of hand. No big crowds, the old school way.

Dom is my brother from another mother. We live 120 miles apart but are there for each other and always will be.

I haven't met many men like Dom or myself. We are good men, loving fathers, very protective and honourable. We have integrity and we are still old school.

If you want to see Dom or me really p*ss*d off, cross our daughters Bella and Mia - then it's a different story which can't be printed. Otherwise, we're just loving old school dads.

GARY BEAZLEY
(Former Security Colleague)

I met Dom late 1989/1990, working at a company called Top Guard, which was run by Kevin Camp and he had his brother John Camp, we all know him as Jonny Fast Hands. We worked together for about one and a half years.

Thanks to the likes of Dom and Kevin who first trained me up to do it. Because I had never done door work until I met them. I was only 23/24, Never done a door in me life.

I remember my first interview was with Kevin Camp and Dave in a little office. We kind of jelled together on the interview and before I got home, they had phoned me. I went in on the Thursday and was working on the Friday - a rock night at the Astoria.

It was my first taste at doing door work, meeting all new let's say interesting people, from all walks of life and backgrounds and that.

The first time I was introduced to Dom, I was told to meet him and bring him down to a club called the Venue in New Cross which was pretty much where I spent most of my time working with Dom.

When I first heard about this guy, he was "gonna make it good". Good boxer, calm nature and everything. I was like ok, ok. We met up and we went down to the club. It was one of the clubs, how would you say it, it was very lively. A very lively atmosphere. It was all walks of life. It used to be an old Irish club, it had all traditional Irish bands and all that. Then the son and daughter I believe took over the club, it was the new starting era of the Indie come Fresh Metal Punky sort of thing.

So, we had all these sorts of lively characters coming down with a mixture of the old Irish. Sometimes it didn't go down to well. There was a bit of clashing on the doors.

I remember one night, they used to have a bar right at the top and a fight had broken out there. There was about 150/200 steps to the top bar running through the club. It was up three floors. Dom was already going at it hammer and tongs. He was on his own in the beginning if I remember rightly. This guy who I saw at the beginning of the night, who kind of reminded me of the little old Milky Bar Kid, which we made his nickname, how can you explain this.

He was fiery. Fiery, but he also had a good calming way when you worked with him, you kind of worked together as a team. It was like the good and bad cops, the ones at the front calmer/talkers, and the handier ones.

At the venue we had quite a few rough nights, I will be careful how I put this… Back in those days' doormen were doormen. I consider doormen nowadays to be pin cushions because how it was back then for us. We were looking after quite a few troublesome clubs but it was done in a professional menacing way. We protected the customers that were in there and wanted to enjoy themselves, but obviously you got your wrongens in there which quickly got dealt with.

We were notorious for going in and getting rid of things like that, in our own way as a team. But we also had the other doormen, that would be the talkers, so they would talk and calm it down.

Most of the times my memories of Dom was (laughing) he wasn't always a good talker. We used to have another guy Matt, I believe his name was. He was the talker and Dom wasn't.

Another memory is we were going up to Swansea and we was going to Portsmouth. We were doing the rave scene all over the place. We were doing Fantasia which was the first 25,000 ticket back in 1993. You have got to be able to trust each and every one of your team. Do I trust Dom with my life, yes I do!!!! When you are working with Dom, he is your shadow. He has got your back, that's if he ain't in front of ya lol.

He is a hard one to calm down afterwards. There was probably 15/20 hard core Mick the Greek, Dave Anderson god rest his soul. You had Mark Camp he was a bit more on the outskirts of it. You had Tall Terry, he is in Australia now. John Novo, there was another guy Adam Rossiter, Little Mick aka Raff the Staff we used to call him at the Hacienda. A nice crowd of us, even though we are all old fogies now. We all still keep in touch with each other and still share the memories. Probably some of the most fantastic nights on door work and working with a team like that I have ever done.

The rest as they say is history - distant memory

About 1993 Dom made it a bit bigger and went further up and down the country looking after the bands and things like that. I left the company and went on my own, and done my own thing, working in other clubs, doors with other teams. We always, how could you say it, we always had that loyalty to one another, everyone was always at the end of a phone call. It didn't matter where you was. That's what I loved about Dom, Kevin, John, no matter where you was, it wasn't about like what you see it now.

Now it is more about gangs. It wasn't like that back then, we all looked out for each other, helped each other out. Whether it would have been financially, through our contacts, extra work, everyone became like family. Everyone looked out for each other. Dom was very good at that, helping out, looking after his friends, the close knit.

Like I said after a few years Dom went further into the field and a bit more up there than me.

Since I spoke with Dom, which was recently, and him saying he wanted me to say certain stories from the past, I thought I don't want to get anyone into trouble lol, its history. People have this thing of wanting to rewrite history, and there are certain things that you just can't do. Dom might have been there but not taken the lead role, and I wouldn't want to get someone else into trouble.

With Dom as a friend, wow, he is one of a kind. He has always been there. We have always kept this thing up. Even though we don't see each other often, for three years, then all of a sudden it's like you not been away from him. You know what I mean, it's a great big bear hug and like an old session of the history that comes up.

We all have a laugh and a giggle and it's a friendship with Dom that you don't feel you have missed out 10 years of time, it's like he has been there all the time. That's my off the top of the head memories of him.

He also trained one of my sons when he was 11, he wanted to have a go at boxing. I got in touch with Dom and he trained him for a year or so and had his first exhibition under Dom. Dom was in his corner. He was quite good but lost the love of boxing and has gone into Mai Tai.

COLIN MANNERS
(Former Top Professional Fighter)

I don't know Dominic personal, personal, personal. But I know of Dominic's reputation on the boxing scene and unfortunately I know of his reputation on the gangland scene as well. A very respected enforcer and how can I put it, he gets the job done.

One thing I can't do and I find it very hard is to give information on anybody because it is against my grain.

What I will say honestly is Dominic Negus has changed and to a degree I think the biggest effect that I can think that he had on his life was his daughter. And I think as his daughter got that little bit older, close to her fours and fives, I think he actually started to realise that there are things that he could be threatened with that could affect him and the decision and judgements he made, because in reality Dominic was quite ruthless.

He could read a situation, smell trouble and sort it out, you know what I mean, as simple as that, from my reckoning.

Dominic is a caged polar bear, you know what they do? You can't fuck about with a polar bear in their own domain you know. That fucker will hunt you down. Will smell you from a fucking mile away and he will hunt you down and keep going, going, going. You can't outrun or get away from a polar bear, once you have pissed them off once, it's just not happening.

People talk about tigers and all that, but polar bears smell you from miles away and will keep coming, they will keep coming and they will find ya.

With Dom when the weakness came, what I mean is the weakness in his armour came when he considered his daughter and how she might be affected and how she might look at him. I think from my point of view the biggest turning point in his life wasn't a threat from another man or another firm, it was always in his conscience knowing that at some point in time he had to be a father to his daughter. For me that is a mark of the man.

Having Tom, Dick or Harry being fearful of him. He could walk into a room and people shivered so to speak and wondered what was going on. But he changed his life and turned it around and went "You know what, I have got nothing without the love and respect from my daughter and be able to go from A to Z".

We were talking recently, me and Dominic and we was talking about how difficult it is, actually expressing what you have done because there is a lot of cracked heads and bust lips out there, if you know what I mean. They may have healed but the memories, the memories are very long and if you are in that kind of dog eat dog world, you know what you have to remember your enemies and you have to remember there may always be a come-back.

I know that this might not be the most exciting thing you hear in your stories of Dominic Negus, but I come with the reality of it.

I am not one of them that can tell you how he split somebody's head and knocked out 17 geezers and this, that and the other. But I can tell you that from my network and

160

the people that I know, Dominic was a serious threat and a good man to employ to get your money back.

What I say is, this is how I speak and see it about Dominic. I am getting a book done and me and Dominic were talking and saying look in certain respects we have to remember that we have cracked a few heads in our time. Listen I've done nought compared to Dominic. I know what Dominic has done. (Even with my book I have to be a little bit aware and conscious of the fact that there might be people out there who also remember me).

Dominic is one of the lucky ones in as much as he was able to change his life. There is a lot of people that don't get to do that. There are some serious, seriously dangerous men who didn't get out in time, and have ended up dead. Where he has got out in time and has got enough about him and enough respect and enough sense that he can actually walk away from them. The heads that he cracked, they deserved to be cracked as so to speak. I can't say no more than that.

BIG GAZ GREEN
(Security Colleague)

Me and Dom started working together around 2010. We were working for a company called MAN Commercial and we were bodyguards for the boxing. For the fighters, ring walking. That was the first time I met him.

I had obviously heard of Dominic, I knew what he was about from the Danny Dyer Deadliest Men programme. I know he was a bit of a geezer. Was told to be a bit careful round him.

Sometimes he can be as happy as Larry and the next day as cold as ice sort of thing.

I have seen him flip his lid a few times, get a big upset with people, obviously within security at the boxing. He is a very very handy guy that you would want around you.

I always felt very very safe in his presence and all the fighters were very safe in his presence as well because

161

obviously everyone knew what he was about, he could look after himself being an ex-fighter.

He was a great lad and as I said there were different moods to him.

There is stuff where he has lost the plot, but I can't go into detail on that, because I don't think it's appropriate.

He came down to see me recently and we did a pod cast. We talked about a load of things. The podcast is on You Tube called Talk2Gaz.

Big Teddy Bear A TRUE FRIEND ONE HARD CUNT
GREAT PERSONALITY
PERSONABLE TRUSTWORTHY BIG OLD CUDDLY TEDDY BEAR
A PROPER MAN LOYALTY
RESPECTFUL NOT TO BE FUCKED WITH LOL
OLD SCHOOL LOYALTY
MISERABLE FUCKER DANGEROUS
Big Bear BIG LUMP
HAPPIEST
COURAGE KINDNESS PERSON FRIENDSHIP
IN THE
WORLD RESPECTFUL
CAGED POLAR BEAR
HEART OF GOLD
BIG CHARACTER HUGE SMILE
STRENGTH
The Best Father LOVELY BUT SCARY
I LOVE HIM
FIERCELY LOYAL
Don't Take His Kindness For Weakness GENTLEMAN

FRIENDS

"Every day of the week"

RICKY HATTON MBE
(Unified Light-welterweight World Champion)

I must have been about 18/19 years of age when I first met Dom, it was 1997. I was turning professional with Frank Warren at the time and Dominic was doing all the security. It's known in boxing I haven't always got on with them, but the minute I met Dom we just hit it off.

He was the one who physically used to walk me in for all me fights and was in the changing room when all the security was there. He was always "How you Ricky? You alright? You gonna be great tonight son, don't worry about it". You know as a youngster it was a good help. It was a team, Frank Warren, Sky Sports and who Dom worked for, we became a bit of a family in many respects and Dom was the one I ended up hitting it off with most.

He is a larger than life character, a right laugh a minute. We both had similar sense of humours that made us get on great and we stayed mates ever since.

I live in Manchester and he lives down South so I don't see him too often these days and it can go time to time when we don't speak, but he will drop me a call or a text to see how I'm doing – we have had a great relationship over the years.

He used to train Boy Jones Junior. He used to bring Ben down to spar with me and I used to take the mickey out of him and say "Dom fancy doing a few rounds?" and it'd be the same with him "Fancy doing a few rounds?" and I'd reply "I can't mate, I don't want to give me weight away, and that's coming from Ricky Hatton, that's saying something I mean Ricky Fatton, I beg your pardon". I was known as Ricky Fatton and Dom is a big lad.

164

He is a gentleman, one of boxings gentleman, but you wouldn't wanna mess with him or get on the wrong side of Dom.

I remember he boxed at an unlicensed boxing match with a really good friend of mine called Chris Bacon, an Australian guy from Manchester, it was horrible. Sometimes it happens in boxing, as I said we are a family and all that in boxing, but sometimes it happens that your mates end up fighting each other. I'm sure Dom has been in the same situation where you have to stand there and watch a couple of your mates fight each other. I had to stand and watch Dom and Chris. It was at the Ritz in Manchester. Unfortunately, Dom got beat that night by Chris. But Chris is a gentleman like Dom, it was a hell of a fight, a right ding dong, but Dom came second best in that.

It's the only sport in the world where you knock chunks out of each other, then because of the respect you become mates, mates for life. Chris had become mates with Dom just like I had.

I have seen him cry. This just shows the friendship that we have. Even though you wouldn't want to cross him, you wouldn't want to get on the wrong side of Dom. That's why we love him. He is a hard man but he is a gentleman with a lovely soft side to him.

I remember Dom had a 40th down in London. I said to Chris lets tell Dom we can't make it but we will go down and surprise him. We both told Dom we couldn't make it as we already had something on. Dom was like "oh ok, never mind". We knew where and what time it was and all that and just as they were singing happy birthday to him, me and Chris walk through the door and went "HEEEEEY".

You know for a big hard man he shed a few fucking tears that night. I tell you. He started crying with emotion. I'd like to think it made his birthday. We took him by surprise. Not many people see Dom cry but Ricky Hatton and Chris Bacon were two of them.

It's very kind that he calls me the Peoples Champion. It makes me feel lovely. Dom has had an up and down life and been involved in boxing for all these years, and he was a security guard working for Frank Warren, so I mean out of the champions he has walked into the ring over the years, the World Champions and God knows how many fighters. For Dom to say Ricky Hatton is the Peoples Champion, makes me feel very very proud.

When I look at him I don't see a Mr Nasty, I am one of the fortunate that have seen the other side to him.

DAVE LEWIS
(Former Manager and Promoter)

I have been involved in combat sports since 1989, and at the time I first met Dominic, I was working in professional boxing in the United Kingdom. In the mid-1990s Dom was working for a company called Top Guard, which provided security for most of the big promoters.

I first got introduced to him at an event in York Hall, and we started chatting. I remember him telling me that he was on the verge of turning professional. We got along well and became friends from there. We happened to be living in the same area at the time and realized that we had several mutual acquaintances, which coincided with us meeting socially.

A group of us used to travel abroad quite often—places like the Canaries, Italy, San Francisco, and Las Vegas for the Hamed vs. Barrera fight. Despite being occasionally boisterous, the trips were always enjoyable. We had plenty of laughs, a lot of drinking, and a lot of fun. It was 20+ years ago now, so you are bound to forget half of what went on, but you know you really enjoyed it.

Unfortunately, we don't get to see each other as much as we would like these days, but when I do bump into Dom, we always have a laugh and reminisce about the good old days.

From a professional perspective, I was fortunate to be able to assist him in his career. He was looking for a new promoter, and I was able to connect him with a guy from South Africa who was promoting in the UK. He promoted his last seven fights (including the Southern Area and WBU

166

Titles), culminating in the Audley Harrison fight, which has been well documented.

Audley's manager/agent at the time was Colin McMillan, a former world champion. He reached out to me and said, "Audley has got a fight coming up, would Dominic be interested?" The fight was made within a couple of days. Dominic was not concerned with the money; he was simply interested in fighting. A fight can be easily be made if both parties want it, which they did. Thankfully, I was able to assist with that too.

He can be a complicated person, but deep down he is very sensitive, even though he doesn't show it that often.

He is a good friend.

RAY RAY COLEMAN
(Friend)

I have known Dom for 20 years, I can't remember how I first met him but it must have been through the boxing world. He turned over as a pro boxer many years ago and then boxed under the IBA which I do the judging on the shows, and have done for many years.

Once you meet him you never forget him. He is larger than life and we struck up a good relationship.

We have been away on holiday and he has lived with me for a period of time. We go back many years and get together whenever we possibly can.

One year we went to Spain on holiday. Dominic is quite recognised wherever you go. He was always fun to be around. Quite a few people wanted a photograph with him or an autograph. I remember one time we went out to watch a fight in Germany. It was David Haye/Glicko fight, and we drove out there. There were six of us out there. It was 600 miles more than our co driver said it would be so it took us a lot longer than expected. We just about got there for the fight. Literally spent a few hours in Germany, got back in the car and had to drive home.

Even there people recognised Dom, he was pretty well known for his fight with Audley Harrison, so a lot of people remember the fight. I'm surprised he didn't get disqualified from that fight, because even though Audley was doing his dirty tactics, Dom did get up and head butt him which was not in the rules of boxing. He was pretty well remembered for that.

Dom was always polite, and would talk to anybody. Sometimes you think good god Dominic you gotta stop talking. We gotta get out of this place, not sit here for four hours talking. He was always up for having a laugh with anybody and photographs or picture, autographs.

He was always very polite with people until someone overstepped the line, then you wouldn't want to be on that side of the line with him.

I remember another time we went to Spain together. We were both having issues with our partners at the time. The first half of the holiday I kept saying "Dom I'm going home, I've had enough" and he convinced me not to go home and stay and see the holiday through. Then the second half of the holiday he was going home and I convinced him to stay and see the holiday through lol.

I remember one time in particular he was having a ruck with Nic. He was walking alongside a river/sea front. I remember she threatened to put him into the sea, I thought you are taking a chance.

Dom used to sort of live with me some of the time when he was not getting on too well with Nic. We used to go out quite a bit, socialising. He is always full of life, full of beans, a character and a half, always good for a laugh when you are around him.

He was always a bit wild before Bella, once he got Bella he settled down. He idolises Bella. She is the apple of his eye. Everything he does is for Bella and trying to give her a better home life for him and the family. He has settled down and is a lot more responsible now, however, whatever he is doing is always for Bella. We used to go out quite regularly with Bella and she would come and stay over too. We went to different shows and venues all together. Dom is an excellent father. When Bella was little she named me Ray Ray and it has stuck with me ever since.

You can always rely on Dom to be there if you needed a shoulder to cry on or assistance in any direction. He is always there for you. He is a very loyal friend.

PETER FAIRES
(Entrepreneur and Friend)

Quite a long time ago, we were introduced through mutual friends. It was to do with another club boxer that he was looking after. Dom was looking for a bit of help, giving the guy a lift on his way, and I was happy to sort, have a bit of fun and see where it took us. It didn't work out with the boxer but a friendship formed between me and Dom.

He has told me his story from back in the day when he was up to whatever. Some of his stories keep me up at night, to say the least lol.

We started on a sponsorship journey together to get his boys moving forward.

The rest is history.

We used to go out for a few beers together. I tried to look after him as best as I could as he has a few demons kept inside that big cannister of his. I tried to keep him on the straight and narrow.

You know what makes me laugh. For someone who is so much, so intimidating, it's just the way he talks to me and the way he texts me you would thing he batted for the other side. It always makes for a laugh. He sends me kisses, love ya, love ya, love ya all the time. If anyone heard the voice mails from him, they would think he was my boyfriend. Haha.

Honestly, when someone once heard one of the messages, and I showed them a picture of him. They were like "wow, I ain't gonna argue with him anyway" lol. "He can do whatever he likes" haha

He is a good guy. I have a partner on the production side. I think Dominic's life his story would make a great film. A good one to watch if you are into the gritty British drama.

Because all the stories would be true. He would want to play himself though, lol, and think he might be a bit old for that.

His podcasts are great. He can laugh at himself. All the things that have gone on in his life. From the stitches in his head to inches away from not being here anymore, to how he is as a father and how he has time with young kids.

Good has come out of something bad. It taught him a lesson and he changed direction. He always seems to be positive now and that shows he has come a long long way.

The life he led before, he got carried away and when you listen to him, he played certain things down. It was not a place he wanted to be, living that life. Getting out of it is also for sure a very difficult thing to do. Getting out of it and staying out of it that must be a battle every day. It must be easy to be tempted and get back into it. But to stay strong and stay out of it. I take my hat off to him.

Bella is his main focus. I have a daughter of a similar age and three boys, with another on the way. Having a girl, they do melt ya.

ROB SCOTT
(Friend)

In 2007 I was working on a friend of Dom's house. I'm a painter and was working late one evening on the top floor. The house was empty and suddenly I heard this guy behind me "Alright mate, how's it going? You doing the painting?". I turned around and it was Dom standing there.

I didn't have a clue who he was, I came from a golfing background. I didn't know Dom or anything about him, which was good really because the only side of him I know is the friendly side.

I am fully aware that he had this other side, that he is trying to get rid of.

We got to know each other. I remember I went to his house as he wanted me to do some decorating. His front door was open. I said "Dom, you know your front door is unlocked?". He was like "Yeah I never lock it. Nobody is going to have the front to break into my house!!!!".

The house I was going to decorate, Bella was a toddler then, and the downstairs loo wasn't working. Dom has phoned up the landlord to get it fixed. They said they would. The following week he called again, saying my little girl is getting upset that she can't use the toilet and the same they promised to fix it. Another week passed and nothing so Dom calls again and says "look this is the third time I have had to call, can you please get someone here pronto?". The guy on the phone replies "It will get sorted when it gets sorted" and hung up on Dom.

Dom and his friend John, have found out where the office was and driven down there and said "Everyone up against the wall – who's the sarcastic bastard that was giving it large to me on the phone?". They have all turned to the right, down the end of the office was a separate glass panelled office with a swivel chair and all you could see was the top of this geezer's head. Not sure what happened but the toilet immediately got fixed.

Gary the roofer told me a story once, he said "I had this problem with someone owing me money, so I asked Dom for a bit of help". A week later the guy called up saying I have your money, and was very apologetic, but he said "why did you send that Dom round"? Gary explained it was his last resort as you were messing me about with the money, why? What happened?? The guy replied "I was lying in bed one night and he has jumped out of the loft straight onto my bed and asked for the money".

Our lives went in separate ways for a few years, but I always went to his fights. Dom is one of those people that even though you might not be in touch, you know he is always there as your friend. I have never known anyone like that, that is why he is so loveable really. You just know if you are his friend, it is real. "Can I do anything for you mate? Any problems I can help with?" You know nothing is a problem, he will always do his friends a massive favour and would not expect anything in return either.

That's very hard to find these days.

LEE OTTEY
(Former Training Partner and Friend)

I am just a normal bloke, I'm not from that ilk of Dom's world, I kind of got dragged into it, Dom's lifestyle, for a very small period when I was seeing him quite a lot of him, let's just call it "that world". I found myself doing things that were totally out of character for me.

I met Dom 1995/96 at the David Lloyd, Chigwell. He was training with a guy called Wayne Cummings. To be honest when I first started working there I didn't get on too well with Wayne and because of that Dominic was a bit tricky with me, I didn't actually think he liked me and he made it quite clear that he was in Wayne's corner. But over the years me and Wayne worked together and ended up being mates which resulted in me and Dom becoming good mates.

I was involved with his training when he was getting ready for the Audley Harrison fight. It was a massive part of his life and a turning point in his career.

I remember the conversation with him and another guy at the gym. We had watched him as a cruiserweight doing his Southern Area title fights and stuff like that and been to quite a few of his fights.

He got to a stage, as he is physically a big man and we often wondered how he got down to the cruiserweight weight limit of 13stone 8lbs cos he is a big bloke. He obviously eventually outgrew that weight category.

Then all of a sudden he got pitched in with heavyweights, had a few fights and then got the call from Audley Harrison. As I said, that's how I really got involved with him as I was training him to build him up for that fight and the rest everyone knows. In my humble opinion, I believe if it wasn't for all the hype and would say nine times out of 10 Dominic would have probably won the Audley fight and 10 times out of 10 if it wasn't in the ring, he would have bashed Audley up, I have no doubt about that. In terms of man v man, Dominic was way harder than Audley every day of the week

After the fight we went to Reykjavik in Iceland and that was the first time we really really spent proper time together. We talked about how he got into what he did and how people were with him. He told me that I am one of the few people that if I phoned him up he knows I am not going to ask him to do something. He had a lot of people in that world, that would drop his name and if they got into trouble the first person they would call would be Dom.

I didn't want to be one of those people who if they had any aggro would be straight on the phone to him. I think he appreciated that.

It's true when he says a lot of the time things just come to him. I remember being in a coffee shop in Iceland and as you can imagine we don't know a soul there. Some drunken guy comes steaming in. Dominic clocks it straight away as he has a high perception of things like that. I see Dominic's eyes change. This guy has come in shouting and screaming and starts starring at us at our table.

Dom was like "here you go". I was like "oh no", we are just sitting here quietly having a coffee and this guy is making a beeline for us. Luckily, the guy gave me a load of abuse, not that we knew what he was saying as he was speaking Icelandic. Dominic has leaned back in his chair. I have told the guy I don't know what he is saying as I'm English and the guy has turned around and walked out. Dominic says "there you go, that's my life. We are in a foreign country, we know no-one, there are loads of coffee shops and he has to come into the one we are in and makes a beeline for us".

A couple of times we went to Tenerife, I'm sure it was twice as otherwise a load of crazy things happened in just one trip, lol. (I checked it was twice).

We were staying at someone's place over there. The guy whose place it was was back in England and he arranged with Dom for us to go. The plane ride was great, and on the way I had asked Dom how many people did he know in Tenerife. I used to live there and run a gym out there 1993/1994, so there were quite a few people I knew. He was like I know the person who owns Bobby's, we are going to go straight there.

We went to Bobby's that afternoon and I could not believe what I saw. People were coming up to him asking him to do this, to do that and you could see he was being drawn into shall we call it "work".

There was this guy we were with, Dave. He was what I call a seat boy, you know a regular person with a 9 to 5 office job. We started playing pool and all of a sudden this guy came up and whispered something in Dom's ear. There was this other guy in there that was really really starring at us and again I'm thinking "oh no". We carry on playing pool and this geezer is getting closer and closer. I'm thinking this is a bit weird, there is definitely something weird going on here. Before I knew it, the guy got too close, Dominic lamped him with the snooker cue.

The owner ran up to Dom and was like "no, no". Dom was like "sorry, sorry mate" That's the kind of thing that can happen when you are with Dom. We found out that the guy was a friend of the owner. He was just as suspicious of us as we were of him and was trying to keep an eye out for his mates who owned the place as Dominic was there and wasn't sure why. Everyone is a bit suspicious of everyone. Dominic's way of straightening out the awkwardness was to bash the granny out of the guy. That sorted out the problems and broke the ice.

I remember a few days later we were back at Bobby's in the evening in their nightclub. I was single at the time. We got lucky with some ladies at the club, chatting away with them. What I didn't know was, and this again is Dominic's high perception, was that there were some guys that had been looking at these girls as well and weren't talking to them.

I went off to the toilet and unbeknown to me some of these guys had started following me in. I had gone in to a cubicle, done what I needed to do. I had come out and luckily these geezers never made it to the toilet as Dominic had destroyed them before they had got there. I came out of the toilet and all I could see were people hanging off of him, he was throwing right handers. There were bodies on the floor everywhere. A big fight, a big big fight. All I remember is the DJ putting his records back in the box and packing up as if the night had finished and he was going home. lol

We obviously had to get out quickly and luckily another doorman took us to his apartment in Las Americas for Dom to clean up and change his shirt and off we went back out to another bar. Think it was Veronicas.

Dave who we were with had decided to go back to where we were staying. None of us realised he didn't have his keys. Me and Dom got back at stupid o'clock the next day. Poor Dave was sitting outside, was sunburnt and bursting for the loo as he couldn't get into the place. He was not best pleased. He left us to go home early, back to England.

Because of the way he was, because of the world Dom lived in, people expected that of him, to sort people out, and he never let them down. I know people might read his other books and think how much of it is true/real, but from what I saw in the small time I was around it and definitely not being that way myself, it all seems possible and true.

It is completely a different world, a world that people who are not in it would not understand. It is definitely a very dangerous place and way to live. Dominic fitted into it very comfortably.

When I finished at the David Lloyd I went back to university and my whole world changed. I went into the world of academia and I wasn't floating around at the gyms or boxing gyms any more. This was going back to 2003.

I am so pleased that his daughter has been the making of him and he has managed to get out of that world. That was his turning point. He lives for her, that's a good thing.

The turmoil of his relationship with Bella's mum, from my recollection had always been on and off at that time. That can't have been healthy for him. I have been with my partner for 18/19 steady years and I don't think I would be able to handle a relationship like that.

I am really pleased he sounds like he seems settled.

He is loyal to the point where it can detract from his life. There are certain people it is worth being loyal to and I hope I am one of those. I was never going to be one of those that would call him to sort out trouble, and I think on one or two occasions he knew things that were going on in my life he would say "whatever happens I don't care, even if you are wrong you are right, but if it goes tits up we will straighten it out".

I felt I am supposed to be a man and sort it out on my own, why would I go running to my big brother, so to speak, but you do end up sometimes doing that. Dom had liberty takers that would end up doing that on a daily basis. You know they are not calling him up to invite him to a BBQ, they are calling for him to go beat someone up and collect money that's owed. I was very conscious about that and made sure I called him just for a chat.

When I call him now it is to genuinely go and have a coffee and catch up. I hope he sees me as one of the guys that when the phone goes and it's me he knows it is just for a catch up.

Its only circumstances that we don't see each other. Our life was revolved around the David Lloyd as you meet on a daily basis there, especially when we were training for the Audley fight. We would meet five times a week and it wasn't just an hours training, we would after sit and laugh and chat for hours especially if I didn't have another client after. When you do that for months, every day, you really get to know someone.

When I left the Lloyd, our lives just went off in different directions. We did meet up, just not often enough and then Covid killed it all. We worked out the last time we sat and met up was probably 2019. When we talk though it's like we spoke yesterday.

I would say Dom would always be there for you.

TIM BROWN
(Friend)

I know Dom from years ago from Mark Gordon, I remember going to a fight where he was talking/commentating on. That's when I was living in Brentwood about 1993. He was doing the boxing circuit around Buckhurst Hill. We went to a pub, I can't remember the name of it, it was opposite a bike shop. We had a lock in there and that's how we properly met.

He then moved in opposite us. I used to clean my car at 9am on a Sunday morning. I would open my garage door up, and it was a sign. He would come on over. I had a fridge in my garage. He would say he was coming over for a chat and to help me with my car, but instead we would go to the fridge and start drinking. We would sit at the back of the garage and I would listen out for my partner and he would be like "why don't you stand outside you poof?" and I was like "well you go out with a bottle in your hand at this time of the morning and see what your Mrs gonna do". He was like "yeah yeah alright then", and we both didn't move lol.

Another time he came over, we got Keith the next door neighbour, he was on old boy. We got him pissed and he also started coming regularly.

Every year we would take our girls to Winter Wonderland. I'm not even sure how it came about, we must have just said let's take the girls. I remember getting there and it had just started to snow. We were going round on the beers and jaegers. At the time you used to have to buy tickets for the rides. We must have spent about £200 each. We were up on the big wheel all of us and the snow got so thick you literally could not see anything. We had to leave and get the tube home and I nearly pissed me self. Dom found it hilarious.

It must have been the second or third year running where we were going to Winter Wonderland with the kids. I had had a company Xmas party the night before. I woke up in a hotel room at 8am the morning after and panicked because I had had two missed calls from Dominic going

177

"you fucking better not let me down, you had better not let me down". He was waiting round my house with Bella and my two girls. So, I got a cab on the company back from Soho all the way home. I am throwing up all journey. I get home and he is sitting there, it was about 10am and we are normally there by 10. He was sitting there with this face on. So, I got the cab to wait, on the company. I was like, "how you doing Dom?", and he was like "just as well you got here". I calmly said "it was all planned mate, I have a cab waiting for us outside. Come on. Let's go". As ill as I felt as soon as we got there we started on the Jaegers. I wouldn't have let him or the girls down.

JOANNA BROWN
(Friend)

I remember Dom from where I used to live in Woodford. Dom used to go to Woodbridge School and I went Cantrum. We are of the same age. He used to hang around with one of Tim's good friends Mark. I have known him from floating about on and off the circuit and all the different things he used to do, get involved with. I knew who he was. I

It is such a small world to think as kids we were literally living in neighbouring roads and ended up living opposite each other with our own kids.

EMILY AND CHLOE BROWN
(Friends)

Dom was like our bodyguard. He would not let us girls out of his sight. Dad would be at the front and Dom at the back and would non- stop do count heads, us girls and Bella.

He is such good fun to be around and an icon.

Bella is his life. He is a fantastic father. Bells is an amazing girl. He should be so proud.

WILD BILL WHITROD
(TW1 Gym Owner and Friend)

I know Dom through the boxing. He is an ex-fighter and boxed a couple of good names in the sport. I used to go over to the Sparta gym in Chingford and remember seeing Dom there and that's how we met.

We joined together to do a corner for a bare knuckle fighter (BKB) called Chas in Bolton.

I remember when we left to go up to Bolton for the fight. On the way up to the venue we had Dom in the front passenger seat, Chassa in the back and me driving. It was a nice warm sunny day. Unbeknown to Dom, I had pressed his heated seat button, on purpose. All of a sudden Dom starts going really red, opening the window, getting hotter and hotter. Dom was like "I am getting really hot in here boy". Still oblivious to my prank. I turned it off let it cool down then did it again haha. I think on the third time of this happening Dom clocked what I was doing. He was like "you fucker" going mad, but laughing at the same time.

When we pulled over at the service station, we have all gone for a wee. Dom was in the cubicle with the door shut. I have got really really childish and said to Chassa "watch this". The loo flushes and I boot the door, full pelt. I have hit him square on the forehead. A bump literally came up immediately on his head, like a cartoon character. He looked and I thought "Eeek, have I crossed the line here, have I took it too far??". However, he took it like a real man and just laughed it off. That is the character of Dom. He is always up for a laugh.

We didn't get the win on the night of Chassa's fight, he was up against Lawson, however, it wasn't just about the result of the match, it was about the time and laughs we had going there.

After the fight we stayed over. To me it is all about the laughs and making the memories. We shared a room together, but never again. He snores, he farts, he is trying to constantly play tricks on you. I will definitely get a separate room in future.

179

We always have such a laugh when we are together, he is always cracking jokes. He tells the worst jokes ever, terrible jokes.

I trust Dom in a friendly and professional way. I would have him as a head doorman at any of my shows. I run TW1, they are unlicensed shows in venues mainly in Essex.

He really is a good guy. I have a lot of time and respect for him. Everyone has a past.

He has really turned his life around. He knows what is important now, his close friends and obviously his daughter means the world to him. Dom has a great character. He is very passionate about his daughter. Me, Dom and Bella used to go out for roast dinners and have nice friends and family time together.

He still loves to keep his head in the world of boxing, it is his passion. He is going to start training out of my gym and also start training a few other guys there too. He was a good fighter in his day. Tough and durable.

He really is just a big cuddly bear.

CHAS SYMONDS
(Former Boxing Lightweight Champion and Bare-Knuckle Fighter)

I met Dominic Negus through the boxing, about 20 years ago. He was doing the security when I was boxing. I was a professional fighter, and on many occasions he has had to jump in between me and my opponent because I was very lary. I played up to the crowd and would try and get under my opponent's skin, which worked many times.

Dom knew I was a lovely geezer, with a heart of gold, but it was just the sport I was in. That's what I got paid for. Dom would pull me away, would smile and laugh at me and say "that's enough now Chas".

At a fight weigh-in at Wembley, me and Bradley Skeet was head-to -head. I remember screaming and shouting at all his little cronies there. I turned around and said "I don't know what you lot are gonna fucking do, because I am only fighting him in the ring. You lot are gonna do nothing". I then called Bradley Skeet a long streak of piss and I tried to go for him. Dom just grabbed me then burst out laughing trying to get me away. He wanted to be horrible but he couldn't because he started laughing at me, every time he looked at me. He was trying to be this big sensible security guard and had to walk me off and he just kept saying "Please Chas, do me a favour mate, you are killing me mate. You are hard work for me tonight, I can't help but fucking laugh at you, you are off your head".

Me and Dom have always had a great connection, you know what? He is just as real as they come, you know Real Talk, that's what they call me. He is beside me, because he is as real as they come. He is one of your own.

I went over to bare knuckle fighting and I needed to take someone with me who was a bit naughty, I was going underground fighting. Dom was helping me train. We went to Nottingham I think, but the fight was underground. I have never seen anything like it in my life. We had to park on a main road, wait for a text which said 'walk down, do a left. There will be a man standing at the corner, and he will wave you in'. Me and Dom looked at each other and Dom said "where the fuck are you bringing me?". We got waved in, went through these double gates, two Doberman dogs. The man just said keep walking down this underground tunnel. We are walking through this tunnel, it was me, Dom and my two other mates, we had to use our phone lights to see. Dom whilst walking through says "I tell you what Chas, if this goes Pete Tong, I'm gonna kill you after". Lol.

Once in, Dom asked "where does my boy get warmed up?" they said "Here". Dom was like "what in a fucking kitchen". I won the fight. It was like a 1960's bare knuckle fighting film.

Another time, we pulled into this service station on the way to a bare knuckle fight. Dom's like "I need a piss". He goes into the toilet, into the cubicle, was gone for ages, so he must have been having a shit. I'm a bit of a comedian and I was shouting from the outside "Come on Dominic, come on you fucking wanker" and really winding him up. He was shouting back "Shut up, shut up". I'm like "you cunt, come on then". I was with this other geezer, we have gone in, I have starting kicking at the door, you know kicking and kicking it. Dom is like "I'm gonna fucking kill you in a minute, fuck off". I have kicked it too hard and the lock has snapped. Unbeknown to me Dom was just standing up to wipe his arse and the door has flung open and gone boom, right into his face.

I have never run out of the service station so fast in my life. I heard him screaming and come running out with his pants halfway down. I gave him a few minutes and said "you alright?". He replied "you stupid little bastard, you could have cut me head open with that door". I was crying with laughter for about half an hour.

I was in a bit of grief, where I was in the council block a few years ago. I didn't know what to do. I though fuck it, and it is something I have never done before, but I called Dom. I explained what was going on, the phone went dead, I called him back and he said "I'm on my way boy". I'm like "just wait Dom, just wait, it will calm down". But that shows his loyalty.

Dom used to be so fearless and a dangerous man, but as well as that if you know Dom, he is a true gentleman. He has a heart of gold as well as a heart of a lion. Many people sadly like to judge a book before they have read it.

PAUL ALDERSON AND JOE LONG
(British Founders of the UFC)

We have been running Fighters Inc, an agency with combat sport for 25 years. We promoted a show called SENi which was the combat sports industry expo. Originally at the NEC and then moved to Excel in London.

Each year Dominic would head up the security since the show's inception in 1999. The show was on for three days and every evening once the show had closed the last people we would say goodnight to was Dom and fellow guard John. They would lock themselves into the show halls and stay there as the overnight guards. Nothing ever got stolen!!!

In 2014 Fighters Inc were commissioned to produce an International Chinese Culture Festival. A spectacular event that had the presence of the Abbott of one the oldest Shaolin Temples in China. The ambassador was presenting a Chinese Zodiac exhibition which consisted of precious Chinese arts and treasures that have rarely been seen by the public outside China.

No stone was left unturned in the build, look and operation of the festival, so it came to security. I informed the Shaolin representatives that we would provide the best security cover across the festival to protect the relics.

We explained we would guard the place 24 hours but they offered the services of their Shaolin Warrior monks to guard and protect the relics overnight.

We explained that instead of the monks, we would supply just two overnight guards but one of them would also be from the East ...... East of London. The infamous Warrior Monk, our mate Dom.

The event team were nervous about my suggestion and me declining some of the best martial arts practitioners in the world.

Can't quite recall the actual words when we told Dominic what he was guarding, but it went something like "Don't worry about all that Bruce Lee bollocks, (Dom throwing some kung fu style moves with sound effects). What the monks gonna do if a crew rocks up with guns? .... Leave it to me!!".

When we waved goodnight to Dominic on the first evening, he said with a cheeky grin (knowing the priceless artefacts he was guarding) "I might not be here in the morning!!!".

Dominic Negus ...... Safe pair of hands

ALBIE TURNER
(Accountant and Friend)

I was introduced to Dom about seven years ago by a colleague of mine who loves his boxing and Mai Tai. He came in with Boy Jones and was looking for sponsorship and some personal help. Myself and Peter Faires sponsored them for about three years.

We gave them their monthly sponsorship which enabled them to train. We supported all their boxing events and we all became very close.

Dom still comes to my firm and we still help him with his personal bits. Dom has referred us clients and he has been as good as gold. We managed to financially get him straight which I think he is forever grateful for. We have always been there for each other ever since.

He is such a lovely guy is Dom. He would do anything for anyone. As I said when he was doing the boxing it seemed like it was his dream but I don't think it was ever big enough for what Dom needed. He needed something bigger than that.

He always makes me laugh. He always tells me on his text that he loves me. This big lad sending me that lol.

We used to all go out for dinner and stuff. We have been to York Hall, Brentwood Centre and other boxing venues together. I was at his 50th at the Volt which was an intimate nice affair.

He has obviously told me some stories from his past which I won't repeat. We all have our demons and he has obviously got quite a few as well, but he seems to manage it quite well and every so often he will call and we will chat it through. We always keep in touch.

I think Bella keeps him going, gives him his purpose. His drive to go forward and earn some money. Makes sure she has a nice life and protect her. That's a good thing for him. She's the best thing in his life.

MARK TIBBS
(Top British Trainer and Close Friend)

I turned professional when I was 18/19. I first remember Dominic Negus came to mind when I saw him on the boxing circuit and thought he was pretty tasty. I am pretty sure he had a fight with a guy called Gary Delaney and we trained at the same gym in West Ham for a while. He was training as a pro. I'm not sure if they fought but think they were supposed to and that was gonna be a big fight. Also, I think he boxed a guy called Bruce Scott in a big fight. I know he fought these names but I am not sure how he got on with them. I used to spar with Gary Bedford, Dom's trainer.

He had a reputation on the street did Dominic and was a bit of a handful in the boxing ring. He was a really lively character. But he was never in my category as he was much bigger than me, I was a light welterweight and he was a cruiserweight.

He mixed with the British contention back then, it was the late 80's early 1990's.

My main memories of Dom was in and around the club circuit. I was not really a night club person as boxing was my life, but when I was out I was interested in watching people's behaviour. I found Dom interesting because he was like a cheeky big rogue if you know what I mean. He had a sense of confidence about him that people would go "ooooh - let's keep away from him" and that sort of thing.

One of my funniest, and I wouldn't say fondest memories of Dom is when I was sitting at a pub in Barkingside. I was in there with a friend I worked with. This pub had big glass windows. I saw him rocking up, he was swinging his shoulders, coming through the front doors and I say this laughing now, but I knew from the distance that him and the two doormen,, who were standing with each other, that he wasn't messing about. I don't know what his beef was or if he had grievance, but I could tell the way he rocked up at the pub there was going to be an altercation.

I was mid conversation with the guys I was with and I stopped them in their tracks and said "watch this". I

185

guessed what was going to happen. Dom walked up to the doormen, a few words were said and it was like he waved a wand. It was crack, crack, crack and they both went over like skittles. I'm not saying what he did was right, but I just read what was going to happen. No one was hurt and I'm not sure what it was over.

I saw that again at the Circus Tavern with him. I hate to say it as I know he was a professional boxer, but my memories of him was what went on in the club scene.

As time has gone on over the years, we have all gone and done our own things. We have bumped into each other from time to time. I have actually spoken to him a lot. Everywhere I go in boxing gyms or training gyms/camps abroad I meet someone who talks about Dom and they always put me on the phone to him.

Last time I was in Fuerteventura, at the TKO gym a guy called Adam who owns it said "Mark, I got someone who wants to talk to you" and he put me on the phone to Dominic. I was on the phone for half an hour. We spoke about what's going on in his life and all those sorts of things.

I was working years and years ago on a building site after my boxing career. We were just finishing work and these two guys that I was working with were from Barkingside. I didn't know them that well. I was clearing up our equipment and one of these fellas said to me "Oh you think you are a boxer?". I never walk around shaping up or putting me boxing gloves on. But that's what a lot of people do to boxers, they test them. The fella got me back up and so I had a few words with him, and the other guy. It ended up in a bit of a tussle with both of them, like Dom did with the guys on that door. It's like focus and bang get the job done.

The only reason I had a fight with these two fellas though was that they had stuck Dom's name into the conversation as like to scare me. Haha. One of them just said something about Dominic Negus and it tipped me over the edge and it was whack.

I had a good job, I worked hard on the job and needed that job to pay the mortgage, but I bloody lost my job over that incident. Because those two fellas stuck Dominic's name in, it erupted me. Me and Dominic laugh about that story.

Dominic is a lovely jovial guy. I have always found him lovely. I always feel that if you were out and about and you needed him, he would be there. I know that. He would be there for you. Lovely lovely fella. It is always great to talk to him.

If I was on any battlefield I would like Dominic on me shoulder.

As we have got older I like to think we have got wiser and we are lucky we are healthy. I pray to God to that and I am sure Dominic prays to his god.

TRIS DIXON
(Author and Journalist)

I must have first met Dom in the early 2000's when he was working security. I think we knew plenty of the same people as I used to do the doors as well, but we only met through boxing. We would be at the fights and that's where we would spend most of our time talking over the years. You know the undercard fights and the preliminary fights.

We would be at the events early and used to have to do the report for Boxing News. Dom and I would often find anything between five minutes and half an hour to catch up on what we were doing.

When I took a break from boxing Dom and I still stayed in touch the whole way through. We have been friends for I guess about 15 years or so and despite boxing being the common bond, even when I went away, Dom would still talk. Going through the same thing at the same time brought us together as friends.

I actually remember Dom and I having a heart to heart on the phone many years ago. Dom wasn't in the best place, he was really down and a bit emotional. We were talking about the situation about our children.

Later that night it was honestly about an hour later, I was watching Danny Dyers Most Deadliest Men. I had not long got off the phone to Dom the softie and had then seen the complete opposite other side of him, talking about wielding axes and fighting off gangs and all the rest of it. I was sat there watching it with my then girlfriend, now wife and saying to her "this was the guy I was just on the phone with being emotional". Literally the tv show just cropped up and I wasn't expecting to see and it definitely betrayed a very different side to Dom. I couldn't even equate it was the same person.

Dom is a softly spoken gentle giant. He has a huge heart which probably sounds a bit cliched. But me and him have gone through serious separations and time spent away from our children. We were able to talk about that and share that common bond. You wouldn't have thought it to look at Dom, as he is such a lump, but he is obviously a big softie, especially when it comes to his daughter.

ALFIE AND ROBERT WARREN
(Promoters and Friends)

I first met Dominic when he used to run the security for MAN Security for my uncle Franks shows.

I started going to the shows when I was about 14/15 years old. I am 35 now so have known Dominic for about 20 years. That was when I first met Dominic. My father (Robert) knew Dominic for some time. When I used to go to the shows Dominic always made a point of looking after me and my brothers. He would always keep an eye on us. Dominic has seen me grow up from 14 all the way until now. I always got on well with him and built up a good friendship.

When I got to my mid 20's I started working behind the scenes for Frank's shows, doing the whipping behind the scenes, giving the gloves out and all that and I was travelling a lot around the countries for Frank's shows. Dom was always there doing the security. It was always a pleasure when he was working security at Frank's shows, working back stage, He was always nothing but helpful, anything we want and all that. We were always there together, travelling together and I have such great fond memories of it. It was the point before I started working for Frank that I got really friendly with Dominic.

I was doing the unlicensed boxing shows. The late Dean Powell who was my uncle's matchmaker said he could get me the former British Heavyweight Champion boxer Danny Williams, who wasn't licensed by the British Board of Control and he could get him to fight on my shows.

We agreed a deal with Danny and we were looking for an opponent for him. We were at one of uncles shows and I was sitting with my old man Robert, and I was racking my brains and I said to my dad "who can we get to fight Danny?". Dominic happened to walk past as soon as I said it and my dad went "Let's get Dominic". It was literally just as I said it, Dominic walked past, ringside. We spoke to Dominic and he was bang up for it and we done the show.

We done press conferences for it, and really built it up. It got a lot of attraction, the fight, because obviously the Board of Control had taken both Dominic and Danny's licences away from them. Where we were getting so much attention, we had people from the boxing world try and rubbish it and put it down. Some people even tried to get it stopped.

However, we went along with it and did the show at the Troxy in East London, we packed the house out. It was fantastic working with Dominic in the work up to it, he was brilliant at promoting it.

Unfortunately, the fight didn't go his way on the night. He didn't really fight at that calibre again. We was quite confident that he was going to beat Danny, but Danny was really on form that night and actually stopped Dom in the fight which was a shame. It was an unforgettable night and one which will always be held in our memory.

He was very gracious in the ring, he took it in his stride and all that. When he lost his licence with the British Board of Control, I think he needed a fight like that to put stuff to bed for him and let it lay. It was like his shot of glory and all that. I am sure he will have no regrets for that fight and he was absolutely fantastic for it.

However, it was still a great turnout and Dominic brought a lot of celebrities there. The venue was mostly packed with Dominic fans and he was an absolute pleasure to work with. We really worked hard and I remember Dominic coming up to me after the fight and said "thank you, I really needed that. It brought back all the memories of all the fans coming down and being in the limelight".

He had fans after his press conference waiting for him, asking for his autograph and he said it really meant a lot to him.

That is my main memory of Dominic, for us where we had become good friends it was just a pleasure to promote the fight and to get him in the ring.

We carried on working with Dominic, him doing commentary on some of our other shows.

When he started to train fighters, we carried on as friends.

What I will always say about Dominic is he is very very kind, very good hearted. Very protective to the people he cares about, his friends, his family. He is very straightforward and also a very very funny man and great company to be with.

We are now in the security industry ourselves and we been doing bits and pieces with Dominic as well like and we hope to be working on some more projects with him very soon.

He will always hold a place in our hearts.

MIKE JACKSON
(Boxing Trainer and Friend)

I have known Dom for years through boxing, I didn't grow up with him or anything like that but I was aware of him before I knew him because he was a good boxer. A lot of people don't realise this, as he was probably most famous for head butting Audley Harrison, but I remember him being Southern Area Champion and being an underrated boxer who gave everyone a good fight.

I met him numerous occasions at boxing and when I first met him I was with Brian Hughes. Brian knew everybody in boxing and Dom was no different. The very first time we met he looked at me and he said something and I say "you what?" and it was as if we were going to have a fight but we were both joking. Brian was jokingly pulling us apart and that was like a standing joke every time we met it would be like "what you looking at? You get back to London where you belong" and all stuff like that, just banter. I was fully aware he could wipe me out in seconds, and to be fair to him I have never seen him be violent with anybody because he was that well respected in boxing nobody would dare haha.

He would rather get on with everyone and give you a big hug, like the first time he met my wife.

He is probably the most non-confrontational person I have come across. People who have read his previous books would maybe think I was talking about a completely different person.

The thing with Dom is he just wants to be loved. He's a big soft teddy bear. Assertive as he was back in the day, it is like talking about two different people.

Bella his daughter one million percent saved and changed him.

He is not the best with calling on his phone, but he did say if you ring me after 9pm I won't answer, cos, back in the day anything after 9 o'clock was never good news. That was part of him turning his life around because after 9 o'clock it was go sort this or do that, and he just didn't want to anymore.

LYNNETTE JACKSON
(Friend)

Oh Dominic, I met Dominic obviously through my husband Mike and he had been up here with one of his fighters and he asked us to join them for dinner. So, we went to a place called the Fletchers Arms in Denton and I walked in and there was this massive fella, like 6ft odd and built like a house end and I was like "oh wow!!"

Anyway, Mike introduced me and he shook my hand. They were talking about the first book that Dom had just had written and he said "Lynnette hasn't read your book". Dom said "don't let her read the book as she might judge me". I just looked at him and said "what makes you think I haven't judged you already?". Bearing in mind I am 5ft 5 and 8 stone wet through, he just didn't know where to put himself.

When we had finished our meal and everything, cos one thing for Dom is he doesn't take a breath, he just talks, so after the meal and when we were ready to go home he just threw his arms around me, picked me up, told me he loved me and kissed me and that was that.

Now every time Mike and Dom speak he always says "how's the boss?" and when he leaves he always says "loves ya". He is an absolute sweetheart and I adore him.

I don't see what is written in his books, I don't see what people have said about him or what perception people have of Dom, I just see him as this person that has everything to give.

I have never known that side of Dom and I don't want to know that side of Dom, as that's not the person I see. He is who he is and his past is his past so let's leave that there and concentrate on the person he is today.

The Mancunian boss sends her love.

MIKE AND LYNNETTE JACKSON
(Friends)

When we got married Dom was invited to the wedding but he couldn't make it because he had two lads boxing. My wife and I decided, it was actually her idea, not mine, that because we had lived together for a couple of years we didn't need anything so we chose to let our guests bring presents to raffle them off for Tameside Macmillan Cancer Unit in memory of our friend. We raised £800 and without any hesitation Dom made it up to £1,000, he really didn't need to do that.

That's another side to him what people don't know.

He truly has got a heart of gold.

ANNE
(Friend)

It's a long time since Dom had been in our life. He is back in it now which is nice. I didn't meet him first, Debbie and Lee my son and daughter, met him in Benidorm. Debbie and Dom met in 1992. Debbie would have been about 22 she is slightly older than Dom so he must have been about 20. The whole family had gone to Benidorm for a holiday because mum had died the year before and I couldn't stand Christmas without her.

Debbie and Lee met Dominic in a nightclub. And Debbie got so bladdered that her and Dominic had arranged to have a date the next night and she couldn't remember what he looked like, so she had to take Lee along with her. So, Lee went on their first date actually.

I didn't meet him in Benidorm, but they kept in touch and Debbie went down to see him and he was coming up to see us and Debbie was going to meet him in the town and bring him home. I think he came up by bus if I'm not mistaken. He didn't have a car anyway.

I had been to work and popped into town to get something and saw this guy stood at the bus stop and I thought "I wonder if that's Dominic?" so I shouted out "are you Dominic" and he went "yeah" so I was like get in cos I'm Debbie's mum and that's how we first met.

Straight away me and Dom hit it off. He called me mum from the very start and I looked at him as one of the family from the beginning. We have always always had a really close relationship except after Debbie and Dom split up, we didn't see him for years.

At the back end of 2021 Dominic found Karl, my eldest son on Facebook, so he contacted him or the other way around, I'm not too sure which.

Then Dom landed, surprised us here, and it was absolutely lovely to see him. Absolutely lovely. I never lost that connection to him. He came with his daughter Bella who is absolutely adorable. She is lovely.

There was this connection that me and Dom got. It was like he was one of mine, he wasn't somebody else's, he was mine. He was my own kid really. I felt really really close to him, like he was one of my family.

I didn't see Dom when he was going through his bad times. When I knew Dom he was just a lovely lad. You know he was friendly. He used to love coming up here because he didn't have a reputation up here, do you know what I mean. That might sound a big wrong, but up here he could be Dom and he could do whatever he wanted and nobody would look at it.

Down there he was, (deep voice) DOMINIC, you know Dominic the hard man, Dominic the door man or Dominic the whatever, up here he was just an ordinary lad. He would go in the garden and spar with Lee. Lee was a Thai boxer. He would go out for a drink with Karl. The family used to meet up on a Friday night, the girls would go one way and the men the other and we'd meet up after and all come home together. He used to love that, it was in a little place called Crook.

You have got to remember that when Dominic was up here before, he wasn't the big lump he is now. He wasn't so big then, but now he is massive, he is twice the size of when he was in his 20's. I'm 5ft so you can imagine what I felt like next to him. He was as tall, obviously, but he was slim. Slim, dark hair, specs. Totally different to what he is now. He was just a young lad you know. I remember he said to me he had difficulty getting jeans, so if he found a pair that fit he would buy a pair in every colour just so he had jeans, having had such long legs.

Anyway, there was one day he was taking Troy for a walk, our boxer dog. He walked to Darlington which is the next town from us. Well, he forgot that Troy didn't have legs as long as his and halfway back the dog was just totally knackered, so Dom had to carry him all the way home. He didn't know whether he was worried in case

194

the dog would die, cos you know everybody loved the dog or whether he was going to die trying to carry him home.

He is a big soft lump, with people he feels comfortable with, but I wouldn't want to be on the wrong side of him. He is a big soft lump with us, because he loves us, he still loves us and we still love him. He is lovely with us, he is soft with us.

When he was last up we went over to Karls for drinks and snacks. We played games and we had a quiz. Me and him swapped prizes because he got a miniature of gin and something else, he doesn't drink anymore. He had a really good time because he got to let his hair down and be himself, his real real self, because he had nobody to impress.

CHRIS GLOVER
(Boxing Matchmaker USA)

I first came across Dom from Danny Dyers TV Britains Deadliest Men, he was on the same series as one of my friends who has sadly passed away. However, the first time I must have met Dom, I don't know if he remembers but think it was the Circus Tavern in Essex at one of the IBA unlicensed boxing show, probably about 10 years ago. I think I was 19/20. I was down there to have a fight and something happened and the kid pulled out. I remember when I first met him it was like "I shit the bed, its Dominic Negus, the man from the telly". I kind of liked that world and it could have sucked me in, but boxing sucked it out of me in the right way. I went on to have 10 unlicensed fights in some mad places. One of the first people that every accepted me in boxing was Dominic Negus.

I remember he used to do the security for Frank Warren at the Echo Arena. I would always be ringside. Like a little shit, I'd always make little jokes "alright Dom?, any kick offs tonight, it's getting moody back there, you'd better get ready". I used to just wind him up.

Boxing and people like Dominic Negus as well as my mate Danny Horne sorted me and my life out. They were mates

195

back in the 1990's. I was the little Scouse kid and was thinking Dom was the hard case, but really he is not. He is just a big bear. He really was the main man and I realised I was fuck all and I was like to myself "shut up kid. Look how humble he is, you should probably take some notes".

We live in a boxing world. The boxing world is a very very small world. I work in professional boxing full time, as a matchmaker, media on Sky. That's what I do for a living. I matchmake for a living. If I can't get someone to tenner now, who the fuck could I get to tenner now? If I can't matchmake myself how can I match anyone else.

People said I was shit. I knew I was not good at boxing, I know I am shit, but I am still doing it. I am answering questions that I am asking myself. Dom was my inspiration. There is a bridge between the unlicensed boxing and turning professional. He was my inspiration to turn pro. The amount of people that told me I was shit and you could get hurt as a pro. I have had two pro fights now.

As I said we have always stayed in touch. Dom's friendly with good friends of mine like Danny Horne up in Scotland and Adam Bailey who works in Fuerteventura.

I have always respected Dom because of the way he has lived his life and how he has turned his life around. Dom for me has always been someone for me to look up to, he really is just a good fella.

I have not had the most straight and narrow path in life. Dom stays on his new path and I respect that and look up to him for that.

I go to him for advice. You know the drunken 4am phone call in the morning. Remember 4am my time is 9 o'clock your time, so you are all getting up and I am coming home from the pub. I have made quite a few of those calls to him over the years haha.

As I said, I have had two pro fights, but boxing fighting wise is not my career, I just do it for a laugh. I have a job full time in boxing just not fighting. But I do find the fighting good for my mental health.

As I rose up in the boxing world Dom always kept tabs on me. He says "Chris I remember when you were on your way up and now you are up there mate". I work and am

196

friends with some top names in boxing, but I never forget the people I met on the way up, and even though this is not about me, Dom was one of the big supporters of me when I was trying to do something with me life.

All of these other people were saying "who are you? you are just a blagger. You are full of shit". Dom was always fully there, I can hear his cockney accent saying "Go on son, go and have a go". That went a lot further to me more than he will ever realise.

It means a lot that he wanted me to say something in his book as he was someone I looked up to coming up and now it's lovely that he thinks highly of me and I am like "Wow, why?". I am still the same kid from Liverpool in my head. So I must be doing something right. I try and be as much community based, even though I am far from home, but it is people like Dominic who have taught me that. It is about helping others.

Dom does it in his way, he could still be the hard man of East London and Essex if he wanted to be but he doesn't. He is a father now and wow, how he adores his daughter, it is wonderful to see. His daughter definitely keeps him on the straight and narrow. I have always picked up on his relationship with his daughter. I think its lovely. I never had the best relationship with my father so I can only imagine how amazing it must be for them both.

For me, I don't have kids. I have boxing and manage the boxers, the little fuckers lol, they keep me on the straight and narrow. I gave up my 20's for boxing when all my friends and lads were in Ibiza and on the piss in Marbella, I was at York Hall or in Olympia working shows. But by 24 I was in New York doing Madison Square shows.

It was the likes of Dom keeping an eye on me and making sure it was keeping on the straight and narrow and him telling me how proud he is of me and of what I have done, that gets me out of bed in the morning.

Dominic always accepted me for me. He always picked up the phone to me when things weren't easy, he always supported me. The only opinions I care about are the people who have seen it, done it. I have always struggled to take advice from people, especially if they haven't been through what I was going through. However, when Dom speaks, I listen.

When I need advice I reach out to Dominic Negus. He has been in every situation I have been in or something similar and he can just adapt to it. He understands our world. Even though I have not been in the criminal elements of it, I have been around it. It is people like Dom, Brad Welsh, Danny Horne, those people are my inspiration who changed and grew in this business.

Dom was one of the people that believed in me that I had that justification that I could do it. People like Dominic Negus, Tony Bellew, me mate Brad Welsh. His last word to me was "Turn Pro" before he was murdered.

Dom was one of them people who when life was getting me down, because people who I thought were me friends but they weren't, they were just people around me, going "don't turn pro now, you are shit, you are blagging it". I am not friends with them anymore.

I have been called on Twitter a bullshitter, Walter Mitty. I'm like where the fuck are you now?? I'm in Miami making sure the sun comes through the palm trees ok. It may sound arrogant and it is arrogant but it's arrogant only to the people that were to me. The people that were great to me will have my loyalty forever and Dominic Negus is one of them.

My face never truly fitted but Dom used to say "my face never fitted either, but I made it fit, made it fit eventually and I am still growing and improving more and more every day".

I think he is an underappreciated hero.

DOMINIC "JACK" SHEPHERD
(Founder of Peacock White Collar Boxing)

My name is Dominic 'Jack' Shepherd. I am the founder of Peacock White Collar Boxing. I had 30 bouts on the White Collar circuit and have been promoting White Collar events operating out of The Peacock Gym in Canning Town in East London since 2002. I started promoting shows in 2002 and Dom was involved in the security of them.

Spending most of my life living in and around the Essex area it was hard not to hear the name Dominic Negus. I first heard his name in my twenties when I was going to pubs and clubs and Dom was getting himself a reputation for being involved in serious aggravation.

I'm also a keen boxing fan so also knew of The Milky Bar Kid in his early pro days.

I spent a lot of time avoiding the man and if he was in my local bar in Buckhurst Hill I would spot him and go elsewhere. I didn't know him and didn't want to know him either.

I remember ringing a club owner friend of mine one Saturday morning and saying 'Hi it's Dom' down the phone to him and he said 'for fucks sake Dom what was all that about last night?'. When he realised it wasn't me, he asked me to go down to the club and showed me the carnage from the night before that Dom was involved in. Even more reason now for me to avoid him.

Having the same first name there were many times over the years when I'd meet people and they'd say 'Oh so you're Dominic, I've heard a lot about you' and I'd say 'I'm not Dominic Negus, I'm the Dominic who can't fight'.

There was a time when a friend of mine rang me from Kent and told me a story about legendary fight figure the late Roy Shaw having road rage with a doorman and he had chinned him. They'd heard that the fella was a mate of Dominic's and I got the phone call. This guy went on and on saying that I needed to stop the man from going to the Police and that Roy wanted to see me. I interrupted him as fast as I could to tell him he'd got the wrong Dom. I met Roy a few years after that and he was a nice man but I didn't need to be put in the middle of that situation!!

Another unfortunate event happened when someone came to me in a desperate situation and I agreed to help them by introducing them to a family member who lends money. Sadly, after the kindness I showed and vouching for this person they let me down badly by not adhering to the payments. Naturally I was embarrassed and very angry so asked Dom to have a word with him about doing the right thing and paying what he owed.

Dom's style of having a word and encouragement to pay ended with the fella's head being smashed onto a car which apparently the injured party also had to pay for.

One night I went to an audience with Roberto Duran and as I walked to the toilet I heard a booming voice say 'Mr Shepherd'. I turned and it was Dominic Negus. I thought oh shit what have I done. I didn't even think he knew me. Dom invited me on to his table and we talked and talked for ages like old friends. I thought to myself he's a really good man and if I'm honest I regretted making a decision about him before we'd met.

Since that evening we've been very close, talking or texting on a daily basis.

Through Dom's involvement with Sparta Gym in Chingford he has put a lot of boxers on my shows and I'm in there a lot watching sparring.

One summer I went in there in a pair of shorts and Dom asked me to bring in two coffees from the café next door. As I walked in being careful not to spill any of the drinks Dom crept up behind me and pulled my shorts and pants down in front of everyone in there. I'm still having nightmares over it. Even now if I visit my local supermarket and if i'm wearing shorts, I always check to see that they are done up properly in case the big fella might be lurking in one of the aisles.

Knowing the man how I do now I would say Dom is sensitive, misunderstood and loyal. He must not let the past weigh him done. The future is what is important. God gave you eyes to look forward and not back.

Seeing him happy with Bella makes everyone smile.

I'm proud to call him my friend.

ROGER MAHONEY
(Friend)

When I hit upon bad times about six years ago, Dominic was one of the first people to ask if he could help in any way. He was under the cosh cash wise himself, but still offered to help me. Dominic was partners with a guy called Ian at a gym in Chingford, he invited me to go down there to work out and would never take money from me. Mentally I was down, but getting fitter helped my state of mind. I went for over a year, three times a week.

When Henry got married over five years ago, we went to his stag in Spain. Henry invited Dominic along to protect him from us boys (we have been known to play a few tricks).

Long story short a few of the younger boys ganged together and managed to get Henry into a strait jacket. Henry was really struggling and shouting blue murder.

We had spoken to Dom beforehand to mark his card not to get involved.

Henry ran over to Dominic and gave him what for, for not protecting him. Dominic threw the table up in the air and chased Henry around the beach for a good two minutes. Henry still had the strait on. We were all crying and falling about on the beach.

Thank heavens Dominic never caught up with Henry as I'm not quite sure what would have happened to him. No one would help Henry get the strait jacket off until two ladies very kindly took pity on him. It was soooooooo funny.

If ever I were to be in a bit of trouble I know without fail I could call upon Dominic as long as I was in the right.

Dom is a great dad and his daughter Bella obviously loves him very much.

GARY HOULDING
(Friend)

I have known Dom now for about five years, he is one of my customers, I work and manage at Farm Tyres. Over the years he has become more than a customer, he has become a good friend of mine.

I had seen a programme about him with Danny Dyer, who is also one of my customers. The person I see on the telly is not the person I see in front of me, if that makes sense. He is just a nice guy.

When he comes into the yard, we have good chats. We know a few of the same people. He is just a genuine, real nice guy

I have not seen that other side of his past, I will say again a really nice guy.

The job that he is doing now is really nice, it's sort of like rehabilitation. He tries to help people, and maybe through the mistakes he had made he tries to help them and that's great. It's doing him good to be that person, working with people who are coming out of prison and on the sticky path. He seems to really enjoy it.

VICTOR SMITH
(Leading Promoter in the IBA)

I met Dominic about 2002/2003 when I just started out with the IBA doing unlicensed fights and Dominic had just come away from being professional. I had had about 14 unlicensed fights and only lost one.

Dominic was working out of a little gym just off Chingford with Ian Wilson. This must have been about 2003/3004. It was probably the best gym I have ever been to. It was literally a dirty, grubby little hut with a ring in the corner, a couple of bags hanging up. The coldest showers, it was absolutely freezing cold, the water used to dribble out. The showers were a shed bit on the side, I really remember that. You had to make sure you wore shoes to get to it. You wouldn't have wanted to have stayed there on your own overnight.

I used to go to that gym and have a proper proper laugh. We loved it there. It had the best atmosphere and energy in there.

The one thing with me and Dominic is that we always had really good banter, all the way through.

Dominic is one of the fighters I have never sparred with. We are both very ferocious fighters and we have always agreed, without agreeing, that we would never fight/spar each other.

One day when I was training down there I remember Dominic calling me in and telling me there are some guys here that want you for your next fight. I was like "no problem". I walked in and there was a guy called Vinny Lopez. I will never forget, a big lump. It was like "do you want to fight?" and I said "Of course I will". Dominic said "cool, its organised/done". I went onto fight him at Camden Palace. I beat him. Dominic was in my corner. In the other corner was Mark Potter, God rest his soul. It was a rivalry but a friendly fight.

After that Dominic and Ian moved to Sparta gym down in Chingford Rugby Club.

I can remember Dom being at the counter once and this guy came in. I have forgotten his name now. Something happened and Dominic picked his pen up. I knew he was going to stab him with the pen. I went over, nobody wanted this argument, no one would go over there, only I did. I stood in between them, as I said I knew exactly what he was going to do, but I quickly stopped that.

About 10/11 years ago I opened my own gym in Epping. I am a manager now, professional coach and promoter. I'm on the British Boxing Board of Control. I have 14 fighters that I manage.

I went from being a fighter, I had 27 unlicensed and only lost one. I turned pro at 28 and had five fights, but to be honest it was too late for me. I went back to the unlicensed again, which felt like home, had four more fights then retired.

I always see Dominic out and about at boxing. His knowledge is second to none. He recently met up with my 14 boys and they were all so engrossed with his stories, his knowledge. He really is one of those people you like to have around with his great advice and energy

Dominic is one funny guy. He does have a vulnerable side too. Sometimes he struggles. One minute you have one Dominic, in the gym bubbly, full of beans just wanting to get everyone going, get the camaraderie going. Then you can get the angry Dominic, the one people want to swerve away from.

As long as you get the good Dominic you can have such a great laugh. If you get the other one, you just have to leave him by himself and let him get his chip off and do his own thing.

Me and Dominic have never had a cross word ever. We are very similar. Very fiery people. If we did have an argument it would be a war. That is why we have never gone there. We both have mutual respect.

I also remember his 40th birthday, that was a great one. We were down in Chingford. Ricky Hatton, Chris Bacon (or Crispy Bacon) as we call him. They had come down from Manchester. It was a great night. I don't really drink, but that night I had a couple too many. Where I was with Ricky, Ian, etc. we were all doing shots. I was battered. I had to get me misses come and rescue me. It was a great night, I still remember it like yesterday. Seeing everyone. I am talking loads of big scary people all having a laugh and joke on each other's shoulders. One thing about all of us lot is we can have a laugh and joke with each other. We don't push each other too far. That is why we have all gotten on so well and stayed friends for all these years.

Whenever we see each other it is always smiles and belly laughs and doing silly jokes on each other. It has always been like that. We have always been friends just not deep ones that see each other all the time. He has been my friend for 20 years.

He is a colourful guy and a joy to be around. I just wish him success in his life. He has hit a lot of obstacles along his way, stuff with relationships and other things, but he is one of the people I only wish the best for. I am doing a show at the Connaught Rooms in London and Dominic is going to be helping me out with the show, so we have seen a bit more of each other recently, we just have a scream.

He is and has always been there to help other people. He is not a taker. He is a giver. Happy go lucky.

For someone that has had the career that he has had and how he has turned his life around from where he was, he deserves to have more now. He just hasn't had that luck yet.

You know he has a beautiful daughter.

JAMIE BOYLE
(Author)

I grew up as an amateur boxer and in the late 1990's that is when I first heard the name Dominic Negus. I didn't pay too much attention to it. He was just a name, a guy from Essex with a Southern Area Title, Cruiserweight. I didn't really have any reason to check him out.

The first time I really took notice of him would have been July 2002. It was a fight on BBC with him fighting a guy called Audley Harrison, the new golden boy of boxing. Dominic was put in the ring with him and it was Audley's most competitive fight to date. Audley won it, but in defeat I remember thinking what a character Dominic was. He came to the ring in a Free Vic Dart t-shirt. Dominic after that fight got a two year ban, it was all over the boxing news, News Monthly.

When there is an unusual character or if people say keep away from someone they are a nutter, I get instantly drawn to that person. I remember thinking fucking hell what a really funny, interesting character you are.

My next thing with Dominic was back in 2005. There was a documentary called Britain's Underworld. It was a really hard hitting programme. It was a fly on the wall documentary. He was attacked by three people with guns and machetes and it was just like the hardest hitting most extreme television viewing you could imagine. I was just like "wow" what a fucking character.

My next meeting with Dominic was at a weigh in in Glasgow in SECC in September 2012. It was a big title fight Ricky Burns against Kevin Mitchell. There were load of celebrities and boxers there. It was full of lots of sporting faces. I looked over and saw Dominic Negus and thought "fuck that's Dominic Negus". I kind of went over to him. Dominic didn't know me even though I have kind of known of him for about 10 years. I went up and started talking to him and he was just really nice. I remember him being exceptionally nice to my boy who was about 10 then. I was talking to him about Audley Harrison, we must have been talking for about 10 minutes and I kind of came away and thought "what a nice guy he is".

In 2015 I decided I was going to become a writer, and through social media I connected with Dominic and asked him to be in a series of my books, one being Tales of Pugilism. By the time he had featured in about four of my books, we were very familiar with each other and I really liked him, I kind of fell in love with him.

I am like David Attenborough, when he studies things. Dom has always reminded me of a silver back gorilla. What I mean by that, and I am not being insulting or anything. Their nature is that they are really placid, they are such a gentle creature, they like to be tranquil and peaceful, BUT if you upset them, they would literally rip you apart. They are five or six times stronger than a human. Mike Tyson wouldn't be able to beat one of them. They would rather be peaceful and loving and calm. That is what Dominic Negus is, but, if you upset him, he can be one scary bastard, but his main goal is to be loved.

I find Dominic really interesting to study. I love him. I like him. I trust him.

In 2018 I wrote Dominic's book Into the Light. I went and stayed with him for five days and that's where I learnt up close hand that Dominic is a proper geek. This might blow a lot of people away. Inside his bedroom Dominic has Star Wars figures. He is obsessed with Star Wars, he loves Lego, he loves Kung-Fu films, Bruce Lee films. Dominic is a bit of a recluse. None of this side of him, the real him, doesn't tie in with who you think Dominic Negus is, because his character and how the media have portrayed him over the last 20 years as this kind of violent, psychotic, gangland connection dangerous man in London who was muscle for hire.

When I got to know him I was like he is a big fucking cuddly bear.

But don't be fooled, because behind the smile, if he wanted to does lie a deadly figure.

I learnt how he was bullied as a kid. The fat kid with spectacles, a real daddy's boy. He hung around with his dad, hid behind his dad. His dad sounded like a total legend.

I have met hundreds of people over the last six years from footballers, actors, boxers. Many interesting people and most I do not let get too close to me, but with Dominic Negus there are no more layers. I trust him, my wife loves him and if my wife trusts him then I am allowed to play with him. Out of all the people I have come across over the years she is always like "how's Dominic?". We have genuine love for him.

Dominic Negus, you are aware of what he is or what the media have portrayed him as. You don't have to read the small print to see what Dominic Negus is. Big, 6ft 2, broad, broken nose, extremely cockney. You approach with caution. But all Dominic wants is to be loved.

Don't get me wrong there is a side to him, sometimes I can look at him and think you can fuck the fuck off. He is moody, he is cranky, he can be arsy. He can be difficult. When his head goes he knows he has to take himself away, because he knows he could end up in prison.

Even with all that he still has my trust. I really didn't mean to do it but I have fallen in love with him, I really didn't mean to. Yes, we might have fallen out a few times which, if you are reading this Dominic, it was always your fault haha, but I always know I am going to go back to him because he really is a good egg.

I think Dominic Negus should be a lot more famous than he is. He should be going into schools, talking to the youth, trying to educate the young angry Dominic Neguses of the world to try and calm down.

His greatest strength was his fighting ability but he was used, used and abused by people. They didn't want to see him how I see him.

In my head he should have been British to European level champion. He fucked up on the boxing, Dominic knows that. Hindsight is a wonderful thing. When he is 70/80 it will still torture him.

Dominic is the only person in the world who came make the word c u next Tuesday kind of comical.

I don't think anything could have calmed Dominic down apart from two things. His daughter Bella, and his age. Feeling the grass under his feet as he put it, smelling the air.

The one thing he did get great is his little girl, Bella. Dominic is the absolute doting father. I can only imagine what he will be like when he becomes a grandad. He is an absolute blubbering mess. When you talk about his daughter he just bursts into tears. We have this ongoing joke, I take the piss out of him saying "Dominic, I didn't know you had a daughter", because every other sentence is "do you know I have a daughter?".

Life needs characters like Dominic Negus.

Huge love and respect for him.

CHRIS SMITH
(Top Security Consultant)

I have known Dom for about 20 years. It was in the early 2000's when Dom was working the shows. He was larger than life and a bit of a character and we hit it off straight away. We had some great laughs at work. We have worked at so many festivals and boxing events together. When people are quite witty and try to get one over on him, his one liners just put these other people comments into the shadow. He is so so funny.

We worked together at a place in Wales called the Wakestock Festival. The festival was for 16-24 year olds.

We were getting complaints about some older guys. They were in their mid 30's, big guys. The young kids were all having things taken and missing from inside and outside their tents. We made a decision that these older guys were leaving. When we got to their tent they were still asleep. We started kicking the tent, they came out very aggressive. It was quite funny really as people were running everywhere.

We managed to escort them out the gates. They were being mouthy and talking to Dom quite disrespectfully and then started throwing bricks and stuff at us. I remember one of them saying to Dom "Oi you, are you on steroids?". Dom quickly replied "I'd be lucky if I was on cake let alone steroids". His one liners are always so funny.

What we didn't realise was that while we were doing this all the youngsters had gone to these guys tent and were collecting all their stuff back. The following day, when we were having a little tea break, the kids were all coming up to us saying "thanks got me towel back, got me sleeping bag back, my phone back my radio back". These older guys had taken so much. We know we definitely did the right thing getting them out. The whole festival was great working with Dom. We had some good times there talking with the kids, a little bit of mentoring them.

Recently Dom came to Birmingham and stayed at my house. He was doing a door supervisor top up course, to renew his security badge. He was just so funny. Even the trainer Dene was just in stitches. This is a serious course. One point we had to do a non-aggressive manoeuvre and Dom being Dom he pretended to be Jackie Chan. It was hilarious. Even though we were all trying to be serious we were just rolling on the floor in stitches.

When we had to pretend to be taking somebody out, Dom just looked at me went to kiss me and told me he loved me. Just being normal Dom. He is just a legend.

We are like brothers. I would do anything for him and I know he would do anything for me and my family.

He has a great rapport with my son Conner. We have all been out for meals together. He has met my grandchildren and I have met his daughter Bella. I have watched her grow up.

Every time I am around him it is always just a good laugh. Never any seriousness. Lots of stories. His life experiences are just so vast. My son takes the mickey out of him because of the Danny Dyer programme there was a phrase Dom said "It doesn't matter if you are Jackie Chan or Bruce Lee if I hit you in the jaw you are going to kip".

He is such a good role model to have around anyone because of his life experience. He has a natural demeanour about him. He is just a great friendly guy. Have only love and respect for him.

He always has time for others. He doesn't seem to take much time for himself which is one of his strengths. Dom always makes sure we are ok.

It's great he has turned himself around. He is just a genuinely nice guy and such fun to be around. He just fills you with joy.

If you saw the person he was 30 years ago to the person he is now you would never believe it was the same person. This is definitely because of Bella. He has so much pride. He talks about her all the time. He is so proud of how well she is doing. He is now pushing her to be the person he wishes he should have been.

The guy is just an absolute legend and such a good friend. A great person to have on my side and a great mentor for the kids. It is such a shame there are not a lot more people out there like Dominic Negus.

DEEP LOYAL GENEROUS

CRAZY AS FUCK

BIG CUDDLY BEAR

HUMOUROUS ENGAGING

A GOOD FRIEND TOUGH KIND

LOYALTY Sensitive FUN BROKEN

REALLY NICE GUY LARGER

CLUMSY THAN LIFE

20 STONE SOFTIE

LOVEABLE MISUNDERSTOOD

GOOD FUN GOOD GOOD FRIEND

BIG SOFTIE LOVING

THERE FOR YOU A GRAFTER

A BIG TEDDY BEAR

"How come you haven't got any money?" "I was too busy being a friend!!".

With Dom it was never about money. Shame cos if it was, he would have been a millionaire.

There was a colleague of mine that lost his job, and me and Dom were sitting chatting to him and Dom said and this shows what a different world he has come from lol "listen if you want I know a guy who will break his legs for 5 grand, but beware if you don't pay him, he will come after you".
It was really funny because honestly I thought he thought he was being helpful. It was said in a loving, lovely way.!!!

I am telling you straight now, on the street, on the cobbles, now that's a different ball game with him. I mean I would put him against anyone and I guarantee ya, put him in a phone box with King Kong and he would come out on top. Absolute animal.

I could tell you loads of stories about Dom, but problem with most people they've already made their mind up about him.
 If you are lucky to really get to know him, he isn't like anything you would have heard about him.
 Yeah, course he had loads of fights and he has hurt more than his fair share of people, but I don't think people realise just how much he has been hurt.
 He don't really trust many people and if he call you his friend then you're stuck with him for life???
 Double loyal, got the biggest heart and is really the biggest kid who wanted to be loved!!!

Seeing Dom fight four fellas at once. He took a few lumps, but so got the job done.

I will never forget the look on his face, like a kid looking at his dad trying to be told he was a good boy and done well. For Dom it is all about being accepted.

Then again I have seen the other side of him, laying on the sofa scared stiff of things that were never going to happen. Such a big heart, but very tortured.

Dom growing up looked up to people like Bill the Bomb, Lennie Mileua, Ray Shaw, Terry Marley.

These were proper fighting men, old school fellas, so how was Dom going to be any different???

He definitely wasn't going to be a brain surgeon or pilot. Dom was always born to fight !!!

THE LAST WORD FROM DOM .....

Thank you to everyone who has contributed to this book.

There were some people that should have been in it, some who thought they should have been in it and some that wanted to be in it ....but it is just the way it has gone.

Hope you enjoy it and if you don't you can always use it as toilet roll.